MARRIAGE ON PURPOSE

Saying "I Do" When We Should Have Said "No Clue!"

DAN SEABORN
DR. PETER NEWHOUSE
ALAN SEABORN

Marriage on Purpose

Published by Winning At Home, Zeeland, Michigan, www.winningathome.com.

Dan

For my wife, Jane, and my grandchildren, Jackson, Naya, Jonah, Shi, Ivy, Elisha, and any others who come along in the future—I pray you will find me an example of a faithful husband, father, and papa, and that someday you will live by the principles in this book so your lives will fully honor God.

Peter

For my wife, Shawn Maree—I am deeply thankful for your endless love and dedication to me, our marriage, and our family. Our partnership and friendship have been a blessing for more than thirty years, and I pray they will continue to be a model and encouragement to each of our children and their spouses as they seek to center their lives and relationships in Christ.

Alan

For my wife, Annaliese—Thanks for your partnership, generosity, insight, and love over the course of our relationship. I'm incredibly grateful to be able to share life with you, and I pray our marriage will make an impact for God's kingdom.

Table of Contents

Preface

We, the authors, are all part of Winning At Home, a marriage- and family-focused ministry based in Michigan. And for this book we've combined our three unique perspectives on marriage to share about how we can all live out marriage "on purpose."

Dan and his wife, Jane, married in 1982. Dan is the founder and president of Winning At Home, and he's been preaching and teaching about marriage for nearly thirty years. He brings simple, practical tips to this book.

Peter and his wife, Shawn, married in 1991. Peter is the founder of the counseling arm of Winning At Home, and he's been seeing clients—both individuals and couples—for more than twenty-five years. He brings the perspective of a licensed professional counselor.

Alan and his wife, Annaliese, married in 2014. Alan brings the perspective of a couple working through the early stages of marriage. He wrote the book *Marriage:*

Five Years Later to share what he and Annaliese learned in the early years of their marriage.

If three men writing a book about marriage seems weird to you, know that the ideas and perspectives in these pages have been profoundly shaped by life with and input from our wives. And even though Jane, Shawn, and Annaliese aren't designated as co-authors, they probably should be. Obviously, the lessons we'll share from our marriage experiences wouldn't be possible without them, and their perspectives have made us better communicators, teachers, husbands—and in Peter's case, a better counselor too.

INTRODUCTION

Marriage on Purpose and Being *The One*

In popular culture, and in many Christian circles as well, a huge emphasis is placed on finding *The One*. You know, the one soul mate who was created specifically for you and is somewhere out there among the other nearly eight billion people in this world!

The online comic strip *xkcd* did a funny thought experiment with this premise: if you made eye contact with your soul mate for two to three seconds, you would instantly know they were *The One*. Creator Randall Munroe used that as a springboard to invent a system of two conveyer belts that move in opposite directions to maximize the potential number of people you could make eye contact with in a period of time. Here is his conclusion:

> If everyone used the system for eight hours a day, seven days a week, and if it takes you a couple seconds to decide if someone's your soul mate, this system could—in theory—match everyone up with their soul mates in a few decades.[1]

It's easy to see how the concept of a soul mate works so well in Hollywood. Still, most of us understand that, although the romantic notion behind it is beautiful, real life just isn't like that.

Now, this clarification isn't an attempt to discourage those of you who call your spouse your soul mate or believe you've found the only one for you; it's an effort to ensure you don't have unrealistic expectations, because marriage on purpose depends on it. Once the honeymoon phase of a marriage relationship passes, we all start noticing what's less than ideal about our spouse.

Peter

I'll take this idea one step further. I think I could be married to one of several different people out there and still have a healthy marriage. When it comes to a strong relationship with your spouse, compatibility is definitely important, but marriage is more about flexibility and navigating challenges together than about compatibility. It's not about finding the only match for you or even the best one; it's about growing together with the person with whom you've chosen to spend your life.

We all have conflicts with our partners, and we all have to face what annoys us about them. We've all run into the issue of differing philosophies as well—issues related to raising kids, or handling money, or the wisdom of moving for a new job. The problem with buying into the story that each of us has one, perfect soul mate out there is this: when life gets tough and these differences are amplified, we can start thinking, *Maybe my spouse isn't my soul mate after all.* In other words, if we genuinely believe the full scope of the romantic notion about soul mates, then conflict can put that "soul mate status" in question. We can easily make the mental shift to thinking we've married the wrong person because our spouse is no longer fulfilling all our wants, hopes, and dreams.

Being The One

If you've found yourself there at any point in your marriage, or if you find yourself there now, we encourage you to rethink your perceptions and expectations. Instead of looking for that one person to marry or trying to force your spouse to live up to what you've always imagined your soul mate would be like, we advocate a perspective shift: rather than expecting your spouse to fill that role for you, concentrate on you becoming *The One* for your spouse.

This book is all about how we can live out that shift and purposefully start *being* that one person for our spouses, all with simple, practical thoughts and ideas that can benefit all marriages. Most of what you'll see is almost too obvious; at various points you'll likely think, *I already know that.* But take that thought a step further—to *But now I need to practice it.*

A final note: We've provided questions for reflection at the end of this book. Whether you plan to go through *Marriage on Purpose* with your spouse, an accountability partner, in a small group, or even alone, consider recording your answers and thoughts in a notebook or journal.

CHAPTER 1

Make God Your Top Priority

The most important truth for a married couple is this: if they each keep God their number one priority, he will stabilize and strengthen their marriage during even the hardest times.

We have to work toward that goal on purpose. It doesn't just happen. That's why Jesus told us to first seek God's kingdom and righteousness (Matthew 6:33). Yet we often find our priorities out of order. It's easy to make work, ourselves, our kids, or our finances our first priority, and all of us have probably done that. Maybe some of us have lived our whole lives like that.

Faith in God is the foundation of what all three of us believe and teach. We don't just talk or write about it; we truly believe God is at work and desires to be at the center of everything in our lives. That absolutely includes our marriages. If both husband and wife surrender to God and make him Lord, then they'll travel through life in the same direction.

We'll talk about differences between the two people in a marriage throughout this book—and we'll do that in depth in chapter 8—because every married person has experienced some level of conflict and disagreement firsthand as a result of their differences. But what we've seen play out in marriage after marriage is this: when God is each person's top priority and each person is working to grow closer to him, they have a more healthy and intimate relationship.

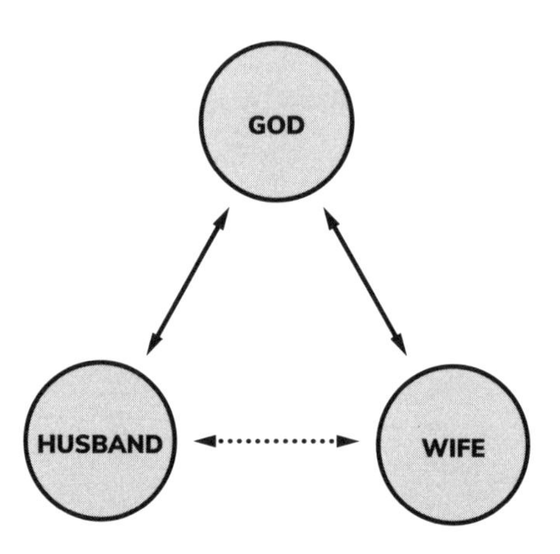

Look at this diagram. Notice that as a husband and wife grow closer to God, they grow closer to *each other* only if they're growing closer to God individually as well. If one of them is and the other isn't, they'll soon feel a distance growing between them. And if one spouse is actually moving farther *away* from God while the other is moving closer to him, that distance will become even wider. That's why it's so essential for both you and your spouse to be on the same page when it comes to each of your relationships with God and your commitment to making him your number one priority.

The fruit of the Spirit is love, joy, peace, patience, kindness, goodness, faithfulness, gentleness, and self-control (Galatians 5:22–23). You'll also find that as you each allow him to develop the fruit of the Spirit in you, you'll look more and more like him. And every single one of those traits will lead to a stronger and healthier marriage.

Praying Together: Inviting God In

Dan

We believe making God top priority in a marriage isn't just the right thing to do; it's the best thing to do! Marriages built on God last. And one of the ways we make him our foundation in marriage is praying together. Peter and I wrote about this in our first book together, *The Necessary Nine*, but we want to focus on it again here because it's so important.

If you're already finding yourself closed off to this idea, we anticipated that. Anytime I'm speaking on marriage to an audience I've never spoken to before, I like to address the topic of couples praying together. And before I do, I always think about the reality that the percentage of people there who will actually take that step is about the same percentage as the success rate with bulk mailings—probably something like 2 percent. That's a strange analogy, but I know when that 2 percent takes me up on the idea of praying together, it will transform their marriages!

Couple after couple has shared that they don't pray together because it's uncomfortable. And to be honest, that's absolutely true! But then I ask them if they ever have sex. One of them is usually pretty embarrassed by that question, but the usual response is yes, they do. Then I follow that up with an even more embarrassing question: "When you have sex, are you naked?" The answer to this one usually depends on the age of the couple. Younger couples say yes, and older couples say mostly. Then I ask, "So praying with your spouse is too uncomfortable and awkward but being naked with them during sex isn't?"

Do you see how easily we can mix up our priorities in marriage?

A note as you're reading: At times in this book, just one of the individual authors will be addressing a topic, like

I'm doing here. Those sections will have a heading with that person's name and when we transition back to the three of us together, we will note that with these dots.

• • • • •

As we share freely with God—both alone and with our spouse present—we invite him into our areas of hurt, uncertainty, and ugliness. Of course, we're also thanking him and celebrating, praising him for who he is and how he's been at work in our lives. But prayer is a humbling and deferential activity. By thanking God for how he's worked in our lives, we're admitting that we don't deserve sole credit for our successes. By asking him to work in our lives, we're admitting that we don't have a perfect plan to move forward, and we may feel anxious, fearful, or inadequate.

It's true, then, that praying together is an intimate act, and sometimes we may even say things out loud to God that we've barely been able to admit to ourselves, let alone to our partner. That level of intimacy and vulnerability *is* uncomfortable. But coming face-to-face with our shortcomings, admitting when and where we need help, and then asking God for his help makes a huge difference not only in our relationship with him but in our relationship with our spouse.

Praying Together: Inviting God to Change You

By praying together as a couple, we're forced to face the reality that we're limited. But God is not! And inviting him into our marriages is a powerful way to grow. Part of the reason for that growth is we can't keep repeating divisive behaviors if we're honestly praying for unity. It's hard to be fully vulnerable and honest with God and then go right back to doing our own thing.

If you consider what it was like for people to interact with God all throughout the Bible, you'll see a pattern: when they encountered him, they walked away changed. Think of Zacchaeus, who met Jesus and then committed to repaying everyone he'd cheated out of their money four times more than what he'd taken (Luke 19). Or of the Samaritan woman who met Jesus at a well and then told her whole town she'd met the Messiah (John 4). Or of Isaiah, who had a vision of God that left him feeling completely unworthy and flawed (Isaiah 6). Countless examples are found throughout Scripture, but even just those three remind us of what an encounter with God does.

Not everyone who had an encounter with God walked away changed for the better, though. Some people doubled down on their previous behavior and chose disobedience. Pharaoh continually rejected God's commands that came to him through Moses and Aaron (Exodus 7–12), and the rich young man was dejected to hear Jesus call him to sell everything he had, give his money to the poor, and then follow him (Mark 10).

The challenge for us, then, is to not allow ourselves to harden our hearts when we encounter God. It's tempting, because surrendering to him often involves letting go of control and giving up sinful habits we might rather keep. But when we choose the path of obedience, we see him work in our lives in ways that make us look more like Jesus. And *that* is a welcome change for us all!

Peter

Because of the positive change encountering God can bring about, we see the spiritual component as the absolute most important component of a flourishing marriage. And I have an analogy that may help drive home this point.

My son and his wife bought a house where many homes throughout the neighborhood were being repaired and restored. One day Isaak and I were up on ladders outside his house, and from there we could see his next-door neighbor out weeding. She was taking care of her yard very nicely. But we could also see her house was in serious disrepair. In fact, we could see pigeons flying in and out of a hole in her roof, and we just imagined what the inside of that house might look like. I was struck by the disconnect between her caring for her yard yet having a significant hole in her roof that allowed birds (and I'm sure water and other animals) inside her house.

Now, I fully understand that finances were likely the reason this homeowner hadn't addressed the hole in her roof, instead focusing on her lawn. Weeding is a much less expensive task. So my point is not to criticize her but to make a comparison to what we sometimes do in our marriages. Instead of dealing with big, obvious needs, we prefer working on the small, easier-to-handle stuff. We go to low-hanging fruit rather than working on the hard things that will make a big impact. Going on more dates and spending quality time together is great, but it's a mistake to miss out on also doing what will make a huge impact in our marriage.

That's also where bringing our needs to God together in prayer comes in. We hope and pray every couple reading this book will take the time to pray with each other—today. Even if it's awkward and uncomfortable, invite God into your relationship in a new way.

Establishing a Purposeful Marriage

Dan

The goal of life is to become more like Christ. It makes sense, then, that the goal of marriage should be the same—for everything involved in *two becoming one* to bring both individuals closer to Jesus.

Few couples today make a unity candle part of their wedding ceremony. I've seen people mix two different colors of sand or water, and some tie pieces of rope or twine together. But when Jane and I got married, we lit a unity candle. And when we lit it, I thought about how that moment was the culmination of years of building toward this ceremony. I also thought that once we were married, we'd naturally (or magically?) think the same way and want the same things. And, of course, I envisioned our marriage would result in the fulfillment of everything I wanted and expected from a relationship. I'm sure Jane envisioned the same thing for herself.

I like to say we sealed our commitment to each other that day by saying "I do" but we should have said "No clue!" In marriage, we soon discover we don't always think the same way or want the same things. And life has a way of bringing things we could never anticipate. Those are two reasons a *purposeful* marriage is so important—when a couple approaches whatever comes their way with both *commitment* and *contentment.*

That starts with each person's personal commitment to the Lord. Philippians 4:13 is my life verse, and it speaks to my own dependence on Christ: "I can do all this through him who gives me strength," meaning through the Lord. I am committed to him, and that commitment must be a foundation in my marriage.

Over the years, though, I've discovered that I should have adopted Philippians 4:12 as well: "I know what it is to be in need, and I know what it is to have plenty. I have learned the secret of being content in any and every situation, whether well fed or hungry, whether living in plenty or in want." (If Paul had been married, he might have been thinking about the differences between him and his spouse as well.)

Paul wrote these words as a man who'd experienced really tough situations. He'd been beaten and imprisoned. He'd been smuggled out of a city for his safety's sake. He'd been shipwrecked and bitten by a poisonous snake. Many scholars think he wrote the book of Philippians while he was under house arrest and likely chained to a Roman soldier. Yet he wrote about doing all those things *through Christ* who gave him strength. He said he could be content in "any and every situation." He wrote not only with commitment and contentment but with confidence.

Even with Paul's determination as an example, too many people want to use the tough aspects of their marriages as an "out"—a reason to break their commitment. In our society, we've come to know that as "irreconcilable differences." But in a purposeful marriage, couples can see every challenge as an opportunity for them to become more like Jesus.

It Starts with You

Dan

Do you see how establishing a purposeful marriage is about making God a priority in both your life and your spouse's? I believe Philippians 4:12–13 teaches us three "musts" for each person to create a purposeful marriage:

1. Your value and your purpose must be found in Christ.

For too many years, I made my wife's life difficult because I found my value in how I believed she was treating me and meeting my needs. Our relationship, then, ebbed and flowed based on how I was emotionally, physically, and spiritually. Jane noticed that too. That's why she sometimes said, "You need to go to the lake."

Let me explain her comment. We live near Lake Michigan, where I'd go to listen to the Lord and get in the right space mentally. So when Jane told me I needed to go to the lake, she was really telling me *Instead of trying to get me to help you fix this, go find your value and identity in Christ.* I always came back from doing that reenergized, and that's because my purpose had been re-focused on Jesus. Over the years, I've become better and better at this recalibration. And gaining the right perspective and finding my purpose *solely* in the Lord continually brings new life and new joy to my marriage in a way I never expected.

2. To find your value and purpose in Christ, you must know who he is.

Too many people don't truly know Jesus; they know only what they've been told about him in culture or even taught in church. For instance, they might believe he was merely meek and mild—practically a doormat! But if they read through the Gospels, they'll see Jesus didn't shy away from confrontation. He faced it. He also persevered through being misunderstood and hated for things that weren't even true about him!

To know him, we need to do what we do when we want to get to know anyone—spend time with him! We might think that means studying the Bible, praying, attending church services, and not much else. But that's limiting how and where God can show up in our lives. God doesn't limit how and where we can spend time with him, and until we grasp that truth, we can't fully enjoy our walk with him.

Not too long ago, God broke through the limits of my expectations. I was riding my motorcycle down the highway, worshipping him in song, when I was overwhelmed by how much he loved me. That was unexpected, but it shouldn't have been! I can spend time with God in many ways, and in many ways he will reach out and speak to me.

The most significant way I've spent time with God is practicing what I call "listening time." I learned about listening to God from a woman named Mary Geegh. She had spent her life as a missionary in India, and when I met her she was ninety years old and living in a nursing home in my town. She had also written a book about her experiences listening to God and being obedient to what he was saying called *God Guides*. I was in my late twenties or early thirties when we met, and she offered to teach me how to listen to God.

For the past thirty plus years, I've been on the journey of listening to God on a regular basis. I get alone in a quiet place and ask him to speak to me, then I limit distractions as much as possible and give him time and silence. I also keep a pen and paper nearby to write down any thoughts that come to me during this time, like items for my to-do list. That helps keep my mind clear. I don't hear God audibly, but after doing this for more than three decades, I've learned a great deal about discerning between my own thoughts and what God is saying to me. And this has led to my being obedient to his leading.

If you want to grow in your relationship with God, spending time listening to him is a powerful way to do that. And as you practice listening, God will ask you to draw closer to him by being obedient and letting go of sinful patterns, selfish motivations, and the need to be in control of your life. The process of surrendering and letting go is certainly not fun, but the transformation God will do in your life in the midst of that process is priceless![2]

3. You must trust God completely.

In "any and every" situation, God is unfolding a purpose and a plan. The question is whether we will pay attention and discover what that means for us.

Here's a story that illustrates the pattern that leads to our not trusting God completely. My wife and her sisters get together in Myrtle Beach every year to spend a week by the beach and hang out. On her most recent "sister vacation," Jane decided to take our four-year-old granddaughter, Naya, along for the trip. At the time, it seemed like the perfect plan. Jane would get to spend some quality time with Naya, and they would both have fun connecting with family members who live eight hundred miles away.

I took them to the airport, and everybody was in great spirits. Naya had her princess backpack and suitcase, and she was so excited to go to the beach and spend time with Grandma. Everything seemed perfect. But you can probably guess that I wouldn't be telling this story if it had stayed that way. One day into the trip, Jane called me and said, "This is going to be horrible!" Naya was upset, and Jane couldn't get her to calm down. Our granddaughter said the beach was too hot and she missed home.

I called and tried to talk her down. I told her she had only six days to go. And then I had an idea—trying straight-up bribery! I said if she was good for Jane for the rest of the week, I would buy her a pink Barbie Hot Wheels car, but *only* if she was good for her grandma. Like I said, straight-up bribery.

Whether or not I should have gone the bribery route, it worked. Naya handled the rest of the week pretty well... because of the promise of a reward. When I picked them up at the airport, Naya came down the hallway ready to greet me—excited and running and yelling "Papa!" I picked her up and twirled her around. She didn't waste any time, though. The next thing she said was "Where's my Barbie car?" I told her it was in my back pocket, and she said, "Papa, you're always so funny!"

It dawned on me that Naya wasn't expecting the 94-cent Hot Wheels car I'd purchased. She'd been picturing a $200 Power Wheels Barbie car she and her friend could *ride* in. You can see how this was going to be an issue.

When I pulled my purchase out of my pocket and handed it to her, she said, "That's cute, Papa. Where's the big one?"

"There's not a big one."

She laughed. "I bet it's in the car waiting for me!"

"No, Naya, there's not a big one. This is it."

She thought I was really committed to this comedy bit and that her *real* Barbie car was waiting for her. So she was excited the whole time we collected their luggage, took the escalator up to the parking lot, and walked out to the car. And then there were lots of tears because I hadn't been kidding. I'd bought her only a little Hot Wheels car.

Most of us would probably resist the idea of being compared to a four-year-old who responded well to a bribe. But I see a parallel to how some of us don't trust God completely because of unmet expectations. We trusted him to do something for us, but he didn't do what we expected him to do or maybe he didn't do it the way we wanted him to do it. We all have plenty of examples of that in our walks with God. But he isn't our personal genie; he doesn't exist to make our lives painless and smooth. Yet some of us hold on to anger and bitterness over what we consider a "betrayal."

In the context of marriage, we can believe God doesn't care about us or our marriage when he doesn't show up exactly when and how we want him to. Obviously, then, he doesn't care about us. But the exact opposite is true. God cares about us enough to not always give us the big four-wheel drive Power Wheels car. Quite often, what he has in his back pocket is sufficient.

No matter what you're going through, it's vital that you make God the top priority in your marriage. Pray together. Focus on the commitment, contentment, and confidence that can make your marriage purposeful. Contribute to a solid foundation in your relationship by finding your personal value and purpose in God, remembering he cares about you—and your marriage—with sufficient grace no matter the outcome. Trust him completely. Marriage on purpose depends on all this.

It's tempting to read these things and see all the ways our partners need to change. So we can create a more purposeful marriage by *prompting* our spouses to change, right? No. Remember how we talked about being *The One*? The journey toward marriage on purpose starts with *you*.

CHAPTER 2

Work on You

Only after you've worked on *you* can you effectively work on your marriage and support your spouse in changing what they are *willing* to change in themselves. As much as others may need to change or we want them to change, the only person we can continually inspire, prod, and shape to be more Christlike is us. Really, we have very little if any control over anyone else's thoughts, words, or behaviors.

Dan

This was made crystal clear to me in an unusual way. One of the ways my wife exercises is hula-hooping while she watches TV, and one night I joined her in the room even though she would be watching one of *her* shows. I wanted to watch *her*—making those hula-hoop motions!

As I was enjoying myself, God seemed to break into my thoughts and say, *That's what you do to people.*

Wait, what?

You put "hula-hoops" around people and try to make them change. They struggle against it, but once you've got that hula-hoop around them, you just love to point out their flaws and the areas where they need to grow.

As much as I didn't want to admit it, right then and there I knew he was right. I was very quick to offer people advice (even when they didn't ask for it) when some situation wasn't working out for them. And that was true whether it was my wife, my kids, my employees, or the guy in front of me in the grocery store checkout line (only kind of a joke). I would correct them and make suggestions! So the next day when I was home alone, I grabbed my wife's hula-hoop and laid it on the floor. Then I knelt inside the circle and told God I was open to working on…*me.*

• • • • •

You probably haven't had *that* experience, but you probably have noticed your first response when you have conflict with your spouse: you think of all the ways they need to change and how life would be so much easier if they would only think the *right* way—otherwise known as the way *you* think! That might make your relationship smoother in the short term, but it would be a disservice to you both. Your marriage would be stuck with a single perspective and some major blind spots.

Instead of traveling down the well-worn path of assuming your spouse is the one who needs to change, look at yourself. The best first step is to learn how to make the relationship between you and God the primary focus and the starting point for any lasting change. Yes, in the last chapter we covered making God your personal top priority and finding your value and purpose in him, but now let's explore some of the things you might pursue to find value and purpose instead:

- the respect/love/devotion of your spouse, sometimes asking them to *make* you happy
- your physical appearance
- your material possessions, assuming they have the power to make you happy
- your level of education
- your job, believing you'll find contentment and fulfillment there
- your children
- your achievements

Or you might think, *If only I had ____, then I'd be ____.*

None of these pursuits are intrinsically wrong, but they're all misguided if we think they'll give us not just value and purpose but fulfillment, peace, and contentment, which come only from God. And as long as we're looking in the wrong places, we'll keep coming up empty. This is also why we must stop trying to "fix" or control our spouses, kids, coworkers, and employees. It will never work.

Jesus taught about the importance of removing the plank from our own eye before we try to remove the speck from somebody else's eye (Matthew 7:5). He uses this comedic image to point out how quick we are to aim our frustrations and discomfort outward and minimize our own shortcomings to avoid dealing with them. But instead of doing what comes naturally—looking for our value in external things or in our own strengths and successes—we need to take the true way forward: focusing on changing the only people we have any chance of changing—ourselves.

How to Start with You

Starting by working on yourself isn't easy, but here are some ways to practice living it out:

Have grace for yourself and your spouse. The great spiritual writer Thomas à Kempis, who wrote *The Imitation of Christ,* said this about trying to change others: "If you cannot make yourself what you would wish to be, how can you bend others to your will? We want them to be perfect, yet we do not correct our own faults."[3] That really hits home, doesn't it? When we have the same grace for our spouse's imperfections we naturally have for our own, we go a long way toward diffusing the tension and resentment we tend to hold when they aren't changing and growing as quickly as we'd like.

Allow God to mold you. When we allow God to help us see our own weaknesses and shortcomings, the possibility for change exists. And when we start making vertically focused changes rather than trying to change other people, we're where God can really mold us more into his image. As counterintuitive as it may seem, as we allow God to work on *us*, we spend less time worrying about what we'd hoped to change about our spouse. We also realize—as Thomas à Kempis indicated—just how hard it is to change the patterns of our own behavior. That makes us much more gracious when we watch our spouse work through the process of personal change too.

Commit vertically. In his book *The Meaning of Marriage*, Timothy Keller points out an interesting aspect of the marriage ceremony most of us never consider—the commitment couples make with their vows. He says when a couple says *I do*,

> notice they are not speaking to each other. They are looking forward and technically answering the minister, who asks them the questions. What they are really doing is making a vow to God before they turn and make vows to one another. They are "speaking vertically" before they speak horizontally.[4]

We're back to our personal connection to and relationship with God. That's because—as we'll say again and again—our life commitment and marriage commitment both start there. But time, busyness, and other pressing needs can easily jostle that relationship out of top priority. If you realize that's happened for you, recommit now to making your relationship with God number one in your life.

Once we have grace for ourselves and our spouse, allow God to mold us, and commit vertically, then when we do offer advice and encourage areas of growth for our spouse, it will be from a whole different point of view. Once we experience growth and freedom ourselves, we realize that God doesn't have standards to control, punish, and shame us but to offer us hope, healing, and freedom. When we experience these positive impacts of obedience, we stop trying to manipulate our spouses into changing so they'll meet our exact preferences. When we experience God's work firsthand, we want to see them experience the same healing and freedom he brought us as we surrendered to him.

Do you see the massive difference making ourselves the starting point makes? If we want our spouse to grow primarily so that our lives are easier and better, we're approaching that in an immature and selfish way. But if we want our spouse to grow because *we've* experienced the healing and wholeness that comes from truly surrendering to God, we won't be pushy and controlling. We'll remember that our own process of surrender was gradual and full of plenty of stops and starts along the way. But the end result was worth it, so we'll continue to cheer for our spouse to make positive changes—but not before working on the changes we need to make in ourselves first.

In his book *The Problem of Pain*, C. S. Lewis makes an analogy between God's love for us and a painter working on a great masterpiece. He says the painting, if it could feel anything, would feel pain, annoyance, and stress as edits, scraping, repainting, and the whole process of creativity takes place. Then he makes the jump from talking about a painting to talking about God's work on us: "In the same way, it is natural for us to wish that God had designed for us a less glorious and less arduous destiny; but then we are wishing not for more love but for less!"[5]

Allow that idea to sink in for a moment. God calls us to surrender, to deeper growth, and to holiness because he knows how much more we can experience if we let go of what holds us back.

Missing the Mark

Paul writes in Romans 3:23, "For all have sinned and fall short of the glory of God." That verse is familiar to anyone who's spent time in church, but many people are uncomfortable with the idea of sin. Strangely, being made right with God isn't a need very many feel. And as we move away from the idea of sin as a society, the idea of working on ourselves becomes less and less appealing. This may seem like an odd place for a sermon, but we have to understand what Paul was getting at in order to see the importance of owning what it means for each of us to miss the mark, to "fall short."

The Greek word Paul uses here is *hamartano*, which Liddell and Scott's *Greek-English Lexicon* defines as "to miss the mark...especially in throwing a spear; to fail; to be lacking."[6] The idea of throwing a spear is part of that definition because the ancient Greeks loved competition—they're famous for creating the Olympics. One of their competitions was the javelin throw, part of the pentathlon. And the word they used to describe missing the target is the same word Paul uses here—*sin*. To put it into a modern context, think about how we feel when we see our favorite college or professional sports team (or maybe our kids' teams) miss a big shot or strike out in a key moment or lose a big game. Our heart sinks.

Paul uses that imagery to describe what it means to "miss the mark" in a figurative sense as well. To act or speak out of frustration and cause pain to a spouse or a child. To fall back into that same unhealthy pattern or addiction again. To choose convenience instead of discipline. We all know the feeling of making a new (or renewed) commitment to ourselves but then falling short. Again. We know what it feels like to fall short of our *own* standards, so it seems odd that we bristle at the idea of falling short of God's.

New Year's resolutions and advertisements exist because both start with the assumption that we all know something is missing. When we make a commitment to ourselves, *we're* the ones who identify what that is. With advertisements, they're trying to convince us *they* know what it is. But notice that these ads don't make promises that actually tap into any deep sense of purpose. They just promise more cheese, lower prices, or more reliability. And they let us subconsciously fill in the blanks. *Life isn't quite measuring up to what I want for some reason, but maybe a new car would help.*

Do you see the point? Anything that advocates for change has to start by making us feel or notice a sense of dissatisfaction with our current situation. And giving us that sense of dissatisfaction is not hard, because when we're honest with ourselves, we all know of some things in us that aren't even who *we* want to be.

So when Paul writes that we've all sinned and fall short of the glory of God, whether or not we admit it, we know that's true on a deep level. And what God invites us into is a redemption story. The first step is admitting we need help! So let's go through the rest of this book with the understanding that the goal for a marriage on purpose is first to work on ourselves—to allow God to show us our blind spots and the problem areas we've been shrugging off as "no big deal."

Don't Expect Easy

When something goes wrong or our marriage isn't living up to our expectations, the most natural response is to look for what our partner is or isn't doing that contributes to that issue or disappointment. But if we follow the model of Jesus and look for the plank in our own eye before the speck in the other person's eye, we'll find some things *we* can do to bring change.

Admittedly, this is the more difficult and more painful way. It's much easier to look for the people around us to change, often because we either don't see or are unwilling to acknowledge our own faults, failures, and blind spots. But if we're willing to see those negative things about us and admit that we're contributing more than we might think to the issues and disappointments in our marriage, that leads to far better marital unity in the long term. What makes it such a bitter pill to swallow is that in the short term, it involves surrender and being willing to be honest about our own shortcomings.

Peter

I call this the 90/10 Rule. As hard as it is, I always try to assume that I share at least 10 percent of the fault when something between Shawn and me goes wrong. Before you think about what would happen if you assumed the same thing, however, I want to clarify a couple of things.

First, understanding that you share at least 10 percent of the blame doesn't mean you don't have to change because you think you deserve so much less blame than your spouse does. That won't work.

Second, it's important that you view the problem itself as the problem rather than your spouse as the problem. In other words, the problem isn't *She's generous and I'm frugal*; the problem is about the need to determine a healthy approach for a shared practice of giving. The problem isn't *He's outgoing and I'm a homebody*; the problem is about the need to establish a healthy schedule that makes sure both of your needs are met. This is so important because it keeps the problem or the issue external to the two of you. Instead of having to debate and then decide which of you is the problem, you can both understand that you're on the same team, working *together* to figure out how to tackle a specific issue. This perspective constantly helps to remind us that most of our conflict boils down to each of us looking at things in different ways.

Dan

A couple of years ago, this played out in my marriage. Jane told me she just wanted to finish out her life with peaceful years. Jane and I are both just into our sixties, so the rest of her life is likely to last quite a few more years. So I asked, "What would it mean for you to have 'peaceful years'?" She reminded me that I'm wired to be constantly looking for something to change. And as you already know from my hula-hoop experience, that's absolutely true. Not just in my marriage but in lots of things. I figure it's good for me to expand my horizons, so I'm always on the lookout for new things to try or enjoy. For instance, I recently taught myself to enjoy classical and opera music because somebody on our Winning At Home board is into that, and I wanted to relate to them that way.

But I can also bring that spirit to my marriage. Jane went on to tell me it makes her feel inadequate when I try to change *her*. As obvious as that may seem to you, I hadn't pieced that together on my own!

So I asked her to list some specific phrases I used that made her feel that way. She thought of a couple right off the top of her head and then told me two hurtful things I'd said. I asked her to please tell me when I said things like that *in the moment*—because I certainly didn't want to be the reason my wife had to yearn for a peaceful life.

I'm still the reason at times, but I'm working on it. With lots of practice and effort, I've eliminated many of my "go to" phrases that made Jane feel inadequate and like I was trying to change her. And I've developed new ways to get those points across in ways much more geared toward building unity in our marriage. I'm certainly not perfect at it, and Jane still has to point out phrases and comments from me that make her feel inadequate, but that's happening less and less often in our home. I'm genuinely working toward making the last twenty to thirty years of Jane's life more peaceful than the first sixty have been, at least as far as I'm involved!

I invite you to join me. Instead of expecting your spouse to make changes, ask them to identify some areas where you can grow and change. And if you can relate to the "hula-hoop moment," stop trying to manipulate or sweet-talk your spouse into changing and start allowing God to show you the areas that need to change in you! It's not an appealing idea...at first. But growing in anything takes work. Think about your job and your hobbies. You didn't start as a great engineer or golfer or builder or artist. But by working on your weak spots, you grew over the course of years and years.

Alan

I've written about this before, but psychologists Henry Cloud and John Townsend perfectly express this idea about practice in their classic book, *Boundaries*: "There is nothing that you are presently doing that you did not have to learn. At one time the things you are now able to do were unfamiliar and frightening. This is the nature of life."[7] There is such comfort and hope in that reminder, isn't there? Anytime we start forming new habits, minor setbacks or disappointments have a high chance of derailing us. In those fragile moments, it's so helpful to remember that learning something new often makes us feel exposed in some way. It allows other people to see our faltering steps. And even though those steps are in the direction of growth and maturity, we can feel far too vulnerable for our comfort.

. . . . .

Keep that in mind as you allow God to guide your process of surrender and the heart change required to submit to him and allow him to work in your life and in your marriage.

Now that you realize the importance of working on *you* and why it's important, let's explore some specific areas you can work on—starting with communication.

CHAPTER 3

Communication: Listening

Talking is usually the first thing that pops into our heads when we think about communicating. But because it's a vital yet at times unnoticed part of communication, we've made this first chapter on communication about listening.

In case you think *we* came up with the idea that listening is important, here's what James 1:19 says about it: "Everyone should be quick to listen, slow to speak and slow to become angry." This verse is a reminder not only of just how much God values listening but that it's his idea. And actually, this verse has two more ideas, each building on the last.

None of us, of course, listen perfectly. Let's see how putting this teaching into practice can have a huge, positive impact on our marriages.

Quick to Listen

James starts by saying *everyone* should be quick to listen. Not everyone who's younger, or who's less educated, or who makes less money, or with any other qualifier you may have used to exclude people from applying this wisdom—including yourself. *Everyone.*

It's essential to make a distinction between hearing and listening. Unless our ability to hear has been impacted in some way, hearing is natural and passive, an action taken without effort on our part. We simply hear sounds when they're close enough to hear. If you think about it, you're even hearing noises you're not aware of right now.

Maybe you're hearing a furnace or air conditioner or refrigerator running in the background. Maybe you're hearing car or foot traffic passing by outside. Maybe you're hearing your spouse or kids walking around, working on something, playing a video game, or watching a movie or YouTube video. Maybe you're hearing other things, too, like a pet. But you probably didn't even realize you were hearing most of these sounds until just now as you tuned in to them. You just weren't paying attention to them before. That's what hearing is. It happens whether or not we're actively choosing it.

Listening is different. It requires our attention. And we hear each other plenty of times in marriage without really paying attention. We're distracted by our other responsibilities or by something we'd much rather give our attention to. Or even by our response to what's being said or our anxieties and fears about what we're hearing. Yet giving our spouse our attention is a key way to let them know we prioritize them.

This is a growth area for all of us. Remember, *everyone* should be quick to listen, but unlike hearing, listening requires practice. Malcolm Gladwell, in *Outliers*, his work on the difference between people who achieve exceptional success compared to the average expectation, puts it this way: "Practice isn't the thing you do once you're good. It's the thing you do that makes you good."[8] What a simple yet needed reminder! If moving from hearing to listening is hard at first, that's okay. Actually, it's more than okay. That's what it *should* feel like. You're learning to do something new—or at least on a more regular basis.

Slow to Speak

James doesn't stop there. He also says to be "slow to speak," which builds on being "quick to listen." When we practice listening, we're naturally slower to speak. Then because we won't get defensive as quickly, we won't be in such a hurry to make our rebuttal, and we won't be offended as easily. Usually, we practice being slow to speak only when we're not interested in being involved in a conversation. But when we feel like we have a stake in the outcome, we're quick to jump in and give input!

Whether it's as simple as saying what we want for dinner or as important as giving input on how to handle a family or parenting conflict, when we have our own interests to defend, being slow to speak isn't usually even on our radar.

Slow to Become Angry

It's interesting how often God's Word calls us to an action we would never choose to take on our own. It's also interesting how quickly we see the impact of our obedience. The impact of being quick to listen and slow to speak is being slow to become angry. Because we've taken the time to *listen to* where our spouse is coming from, we've worked on being patient and disciplined with our response, and we can see the situation much more clearly as a result. When we seek to *listen in order to understand* rather than to *hear in order to disagree*, that makes an immediate difference in our marriage.

Alan

Annaliese and I have found that seeing a marriage counselor is a surefire way to help us both practice what James 1:19 teaches. The first time we sat down on Steven's couch—he's our counselor—we started talking about some of the same things we'd talked about one-on-one in the previous weeks and months. But in those conversations on our own, we kept getting stuck. It didn't always look the same, but the same things kept blocking our progress and our ability to understand each other.

As we started the exact same conversations in counseling, we were shocked to find what the other person was saying seemed to make a lot of sense. Toward the end of that first session, Steven said he'd done much less talking than he'd expected. Having him there with us in the room just made both of us better listeners. We haven't really put our fingers on exactly *why* that's the case, and we don't feel the need to at this point. We just know having a third party with us in the middle of those conversations helps us both practice being quicker to listen and slower to speak, and the result is less conflict and more understanding—our goal the whole time!

• • • • •

When we each pursue *understanding* rather than getting hung up on making our point, being defensive about anything said about us, or making sure we're the one who's "right" at the end of the conversation, we're more naturally "slow to become angry" because our goals have changed. We aren't in the conversation to come out looking good or be the victor at the end of it. We're making understanding our spouse the goal, which *is* the goal. But it's easy to forget that in the moment once emotions become involved.

Having taken a look at how it plays out when we follow God's pathway of listening, think about how often (and how easily) we all get this out of whack. We feel like we need to interject because our spouse's tone or facial expression frustrates us. Or we think we need to offer a technical correction because they said a different word than the one we used. Or we don't view what they're talking about as a big deal. And that's not even close to an exhaustive list. Do you see how easy it is for us to mess up this process?

When we forget the goal of communication is to understand each other, we start to think it's a competition for who can tell the most interesting story from their day or who can litigate their own point in the most lawyer-like way. Next time you find yourself in that situation, take a moment to practice what James writes about. Be "quick to listen, slow to speak."

If you're struggling to buy into this chapter on listening, remember that listening is the only way we can learn what's going on in our partner's head. We've all tried other ways. We've guessed what was going on based on their actions (or inactions), their body language, or the pattern of what we've seen them say and do in the past. While those things all offer clues, the only reliable way to discover their thoughts, feelings, motivations, fears, and goals is to let them tell us what they are. And for us to listen.

We often try to justify being poor listeners. We think if we don't interject right away, we'll forget our rebuttal. Or we think if we let our spouse share their thoughts unopposed, they'll assume we agree with everything they say. We worry it will weaken our position if we allow them to completely "build their case" before we respond.

And that is absolutely how it *feels* in the moment. But that doesn't make it reality. When you read back over the previous paragraph, does that describe the kind of relationship we're trying to build when we're purposeful about our marriages? No. Instead, it describes an adversarial relationship, one made up of a winner and a loser in every verbal exchange. But that's not the goal of communication in a marriage. The goal is to understand each other more fully—even if you don't end up completely agreeing—and that can't happen without listening!

Peter

I've been sharing the following list of dos and don'ts in my counseling sessions and in seminars for years. From a counselor's perspective, these are helpful action steps to improve your listening skills:

Don't interrupt the person speaking. Interrupting is rude and makes the person speaking feel devalued. It's tempting to jump in and respond to or refute each point as they make it, but that is often counterproductive. Like we've mentioned previously, if we see relationships, conversations, or moments of conflict as us being *against* our spouse in a battle for dominance or to be the one who made the best point, we've completely missed what marriage is all about. It's the two of us *together* against whatever issue we run into.

Whether the issue is a job loss or a similarly devastating event, or something as simple as a miscommunication between the two of us that needs to be addressed, when we position ourselves against our spouse, we're setting ourselves up for failure. Interrupting is a big part of that. It's important to let our partner express themselves fully before we interrupt them and derail their train of thought or go down a rabbit trail and detract from the actual point of the conversation.

Impulse control issues and ADD or ADHD can make this especially tough for some people, but interrupting is often simply a bad habit. When we practice letting our partner finish their thought, we'll get better and better at it.

Don't multitask. If you're doing more than listening, you're probably missing something being said. Even if you think you're a good multitasker, you're still going to miss things. And not giving your spouse your full attention will also make them feel like they're not a priority.

I'm especially guilty of this with my kids! I find it's easy for me to check my phone, keep an eye on the TV, or look at my computer when I'm in conversation with them. Instead, I need to focus on and engage with what they're saying. In order to listen well, we have to assume that the speaker and the information they have to share is important. That's what we want when we're the one who's speaking, and for healthy conversation, it's important that we practice that same thing when we're the listener. We know how we want to be treated as the speaker in the conversation, and when we treat our spouse that same way, our conversations greatly improve.

Don't zone out. Don't assume you know what's going to be said and zone out. It's particularly tempting to try to mentally fast forward and think we can anticipate each of our spouse's points. After all, we've probably had a similar conversation at some point in the past. And we know how they feel about this situation or one that's similar enough that we connect it to this one. We know how they feel about addressing this discipline issue with one of the kids, so we could almost predict word-for-word some of what they're about to say. We also know how they feel about tons and tons of other things we've discussed multiple times over the years.

But think about the times you've stuck with a conversation and really drilled down to figure out what each of you wants. How many of those times have you reached a new understanding or realized you were misinterpreting what your spouse was trying to say all along? Every couple has experienced multiple instances of these types of things happening, and that's why you can't zone out on the conversation. Each time we communicate with our spouses is a chance to move away from miscommunication and disagreement and move toward peace and understanding.

Maintain eye contact with the speaker. This might remind you of the lesson your parents taught you about looking adults in the eye when you talked with them. But the point isn't deference or anything like that. It's to let others see you're paying attention to them. We show our spouse respect and let them know we're truly engaging with them and what they're saying by looking at them. Here's a special note for men: Withdrawing when a conversation is uninteresting to them or they're not in the mood to talk about the topic is a go-to move for many men. If that's a pattern for you, it's time to make a change. Engage when you're in conversation with your wife. And a simple, easy way to signal you are is to make eye contact when she's talking to you.

Focus on content, not delivery. Don't get bogged down by how the person is speaking or presenting themselves. It definitely takes more effort to be open to what somebody is saying when their tone or expression feels insulting, demeaning, angry, or dismissive. Most speakers struggle with this. But listening is a whole separate part of communication from speaking. And the only thing we have control over is how we carry ourselves. So if we're listening to the content rather than focusing on the delivery style of the message, we give ourselves a chance to truly hear and understand where our spouse is coming from.

Embrace periods of silence. Allow time for thoughts, response, and reflection. This can be uncomfortable, but it allows both people time to process what's been said and how the conversation is going, especially if it's a heavier conversation.

Alan

I take more time to process than most people. When meetings close with a chance for questions, I rarely have any. When my Plan A fails, I don't usually have Plans B, C, and D ready to go. I need a little time to think through what happened, to see what the current circumstances look like, and to weigh my options accordingly. The same goes for conversations. I need a little time to process what's being said and to think about whether I agree or disagree. So I don't always respond right away, and Annaliese has learned to adjust to that. Even if neither you nor your spouse take as long to process as I do, you will still both benefit from allowing silence and moments of thought to be part of your conversations.

• • • • •

Listening is active and purposeful, and we're closing this chapter with a simple reminder that you need to mindfully practice these steps for them to make a difference. As you've seen and know from real-life experience, listening isn't complicated, but it is hard to do. And even though it takes more work and is definitely tiring, good listening is a way of serving others—especially our spouses.

Now let's turn to talking. For marriage on purpose, we all have some things to learn about this part of communication.

CHAPTER 4

Communication: Talking

When we consider communication in a purposeful marriage, talking is second to listening for this reason: if we don't even understand where our partner is coming from, we can't respond in a way that actually addresses their needs or wants. Once we've listened well, though, we're ready to do some talking of our own.

In this chapter, we won't focus on some of the more basic parts of this broad topic. Instead, we'll look at where couples get tripped up, and we'll do that by focusing on conflict, honesty, cutting out the negative, and kindness. These four concepts aren't addressed in order of importance, but our guess is you just saw one or two you're not looking forward to reading about because they'll probably require some change and growth on your part. That's okay—and normal.

Conflict

Let's start with the big one! Conflict is part of every relationship that has any degree of depth. There's a reason people joke about criticizing their family members but won't stand for other people doing it. That's because those deep relationships leave the most room for conflict, so we generally have more "war stories" about the people we're closest to than we do with anybody else.

Maybe you come from the perspective that conflict is to be avoided at all costs, that being Christlike simply means being nice or even passive. But that's not true. Conflict, although it certainly doesn't feel like it in the moment, is often the way forward. The way *through* the disagreement, misunderstanding, and hurt to get to healing on the other side. That's why positive conflict can play a role in marriage. If we assume things are bad *because* there's conflict, we're setting ourselves up for failure before we even start the discussion.

Conflict and confrontation are simply part of being in relationship with people, so we shouldn't be surprised or discouraged when we deal with them in marriage. For some people, dealing with conflict or confrontation is completely normal. Maybe you grew up in an environment where that was how things were handled. But maybe your spouse grew up in an environment where consensus and peace were the expectation nearly all the time. Whether the very existence of conflict makes you feel like you're on shaky ground or you think you might be a little too comfortable with conflict in your relationship, this is still an area for growth.

Peter

Here are a few ideas for how a couple can work toward healthy and resolution-focused confrontation:

Stay on topic. It's easy to get off track when you're addressing a point of frustration. When emotions run high, it's a challenge to stay focused and on task. But the more you can stay on one topic, the more likely you'll have a fruitful conversation.

Keep it short, and don't be repetitive. Especially when we feel strongly about making a point and ensuring that our partner understands what we're saying, it's tempting to say the same thing a number of different ways, hoping we'll get our point across.

Stay present and future focused. If we start to bring up the "trend" of behaviors that are similar to the offending behavior that sparked the conversation, we can easily head down a rabbit hole of re-litigating issues that happened in the past, maybe even years ago. That's far less productive than addressing what just happened and coming up with a plan for how to move into the future.

Stay positive and kind. This is especially hard to do when you're frustrated, but staying mindful of the need to be positive and kind during the conversation can really help us remember that we're working *with* our partner toward a resolution, not *against* them in an effort to "win."

Stay affirming, and watch your tone. When a moment of confrontation turns into blaming or shaming, it's unlikely to produce positive results moving forward. Instead of using the negative approach, make sure your spouse knows you love and value them even in these difficult moments.

Stay calm, and use your thoughts, not your feelings. This is definitely easier and more natural for some people. But if you have a tendency to respond emotionally, this doesn't mean you need to cut your emotions out of the equation. Continue to allow your emotions to inform you, but don't allow them to completely call the shots.

Stay realistic about the best time to talk. As much as this might feel like a mundane detail, finding the *right* time to talk through a conflict is important. That could mean avoiding nights or mornings when one or both of you are tired, staying away from high-stress times of the day, resisting having the conversation right as you're pulling into the driveway or parking lot for a party or church service, or any other time that could make the conversation harder or more complicated than it already is.

Honesty

In Ephesians 4:15, Paul writes about the importance of "speaking the truth in love." And when we're talking to our spouses, doing it in truth *and* love is so important. That doesn't mean we never have times for confrontation or direct statements, but it does mean the purpose of those statements is not to humiliate or dominate but to address a situation honestly. If we don't start with honesty, we won't be able to take accurate stock of the present and plan to take steps toward improvement as we move into the future.

This also means we avoid half-truths and misleading statements, even though they're *technically* true. We want to be someone our spouse can rely on fully, and we want them to be someone we can rely on fully. That's not possible if one or both of us can't take what our partner tells us at face value. In his book simply titled *Lying*, Sam Harris writes, "Every lie haunts our future. We can't tell when or how it might collide with reality, requiring further maintenance."[9] If we choose to hide things from our spouse or outright lie to them, we create an ongoing dynamic where we continually feel the need to prevent them from finding the truth.

Of course, there will still be misunderstandings and miscommunications as we make genuine efforts to speak honestly, but don't let that dissuade you from sincerely working to get to the truth and communicate it to your spouse well. It's absolutely vital that both partners know they can trust the other to show up, even when it's hard.

Cutting Out the Negative

In their classic marriage enrichment and divorce prevention book *Fighting for Your Marriage*, Howard Markman, Scott Stanley, and Susan Blumberg write about four types of negative patterns that signal real trouble for a relationship: escalation, invalidation, withdrawal and avoidance, and negative interpretations.[10]

Each of these patterns in a marriage cause pain and disconnect. The more we can avoid doing these things, the better and healthier our marriages will be. As you read through the summary of each of these four behaviors, pay attention to the one or two on the list that jump out as your "go to" approaches in moments of frustration and conflict.

1. Escalation

Going from 0 to 60 at a moment's notice, communicating in hostile ways, showing extreme rage (throwing or hitting things, and so on), or being unwilling to participate in a conversation in a calm way.

2. Invalidation

Subtle or direct putdowns, references to past mistakes or failures, or bringing up insecurities about their appearance.

3. Withdrawal and Avoidance

Isolating from your spouse physically or emotionally, giving them the silent treatment or one-word answers, or refusing to address anything having to do with the conflict.

4. Negative Interpretations

Assuming the worst, seeing or hearing things through a negative filter, or misinterpreting or misreading things based on a negative perception of the other person and their motives.

Cutting out these types of communication or non-communication we too often use to interact with our spouses puts us in a much healthier place. These behaviors actively undermine trust, security, stability, and peace in our relationships. And even though they're natural responses, they're not helpful and they're not healthy. In *The Happiness Project*, Gretchen Rubin writes,

> In marriage, it's less important to have many pleasant experiences than it is to have fewer unpleasant experiences, because people have a "negativity bias"; our reactions to bad events are faster, stronger, and stickier than our reactions to good events. In fact, in practically every language, there are more concepts to describe negative emotions than positive emotions.[11]

Kindness

This one is obvious. We know from experience that our words have a huge impact on the quality of our relationships. But it's also important to understand just how much God cares about what we say.

In Matthew 12:36–37, Jesus says, "I tell you that everyone will have to give account on the day of judgment for every empty word they have spoken. For by your words you will be acquitted, and by your words you will be condemned." If we take his words seriously, we see that God cares deeply about what we say and the way we talk to one another.

Many verses in the Old Testament books referred to as Wisdom Literature (Job, Psalms, Proverbs, and Ecclesiastes) are about the importance of watching what we say and holding our tongues. In the book of James, sometimes called the book of practical faith, James writes, "With the tongue we praise our Lord and Father, and with it we curse human beings, who have been made in God's likeness. Out of the same mouth come praise and cursing. My brothers and sisters, this should not be" (James 3:9–10).

If you asked any of us outside of a moment of conflict, we would readily agree that we prefer to be around the people who take these teachings to heart. And we would agree that, ideally, we would be the type of people who do that too. The problem, as is so often the case, comes when it's time to live out those beliefs.

Judith Wallerstein, whose name you may recognize from her work on divorce, wrote a book with Sandra Blakeslee titled *The Good Marriage*. The authors dug into what makes marriage last, and one of the things they found was the importance of positive interactions and affirmation between partners. They say this about the studies they've seen on marriage and spousal interaction: "They suggest that the 'magic number' of five positive interactions will undo the impact of one negative interaction."[12] That is not to say these interactions *erase* the negative comment or act; it's more like they *neutralize* it.

Depending on what researchers you follow, the ratio falls somewhere between 5:1 and 20:1 of the number of positive interactions it takes to neutralize a negative one. In other words, 5 positives to 1 negative makes your marriage survivable. If it's 2 to 1 or 1 to 1, you're in serious trouble. One huge gesture doesn't "undo" everything else.

In fact, doing fewer things that make "withdrawals" from your marriage relationship is way better than a few over-the-top grand gestures. *You just can't offer enough positives to make up for the negatives.* Writing notes, buying flowers, going on dates—those things are all great! But if you're dismissive, belittling, or abusive in your words, tone, or actions, you're very likely putting your marriage in serious jeopardy. Instead, be kind, and focus your energy on the number of daily positive interactions you have with your spouse.

The tricky thing is that it's so easy to go negative when we're feeling overloaded at work or feeling stressed out or anxious about some aspect of our lives. In those moments, we can tend to react rather than respond. And that is often when we do the most damage to our relationships. When we're preoccupied or worried or feeling justified in being selfish, we say things we regret the moment we say them.

Alan

I have a perfect story to illustrate how we feel in those moments. Before I started working at Winning At Home, I was on staff at a church just outside of Detroit. One of my life goals was to own season tickets to an NBA team's games. I found one of the cheapest options they had and pulled the trigger. If you've been to an in-person sporting event, you know that timeouts and halftime are when the cheerleaders or hype team or some other entertainment act comes out to perform and try to keep the energy level up.

This decade-old memory happened during a timeout. The Pistons' host/emcee brought a lucky fan out on the court and explained they were going to play a game that was a combination of trivia and basketball skills. The fan would start at half court and then move closer and closer to the basket depending on how many trivia questions he got right. After he answered all three questions, he would get to take one shot, and how many questions he got right would determine how far away he stood for this shot. If he made it, he would win the prize package they'd prepared.

The contestant answered all three questions correctly, so the emcee excitedly moved him from the half court line all the way up to the right block. If you don't know where that is, it's about two feet away from the basket. The camera zoomed in on the faces of the emcee and the contestant as the emcee reminded everyone the guy was about to shoot a layup to win the Pistons prize pack. He handed the contestant the ball, and the guy shot his layup. The ball bounced off the backboard, then off the rim, and then to the floor. He missed a layup—a two-foot shot!

The emcee was trying to stay positive and thanked the fan for playing, but remember, the camera was still zoomed in on these two guys because everyone was expecting a celebratory moment. Instead, we saw the "lucky" fan put his head in his hands in disbelief (and probably shame). While this was up on the big screen, some of the fans started booing the guy! I may have joined in and booed a little bit too. He did miss an easy layup, after all. Then the failed contestant ran off the court, still with his head in his hands. And in that moment, I thought, *I bet he'd give just about anything for another chance.*

• • • • •

We definitely all know that feeling. We had an easy opportunity to succeed, but we messed up. We said something hurtful in the heat of the moment. We took a sarcastic tone and were insensitive to our spouse. And as soon as we saw the fallout happening right in front of us, we stood there with our head in our hands in disbelief that we did something like that. The really strange thing about those moments is that sometimes we try to justify ourselves and act like what we said wasn't actually wrong at all. In a truly bizarre attempt at convincing ourselves and our spouse that we didn't do anything hurtful in the first place, we double down and reaffirm what we just said. Have you been in that situation before?

In the heat of the moment, hurtful things pop into our heads quickly and easily. These comments are rarely made in moments when our home is a peaceful place. Our zingers show up when we're already feeling annoyed, sometimes at life and sometimes with our spouse. For some reason that doesn't make sense at all, the people we care about the most are often the ones who bear the brunt of our negativity, disappointment, and hurt.

Instead of allowing ourselves to respond with whatever comes naturally, we need to learn to practice responding like Jesus did. He was often in situations where he was challenged or somebody was trying to start a debate or argument with him. In those moments, he didn't *react*; he *responded*. Time and time again, the religious leaders tried to trap him with a question or a comment. And time and time again, he refrained from saying anything he would regret. It's easy to think Jesus could do that because he was perfect and fully God while also fully man. But the fact that he handled these situations the right way shows that it's possible for us to do the same. Even when we're annoyed, or we're being challenged, or we're overwhelmed by other things, we can learn from Jesus's approach and respond rather than react.

Choosing to be disciplined in how we speak to our spouse takes effort and intentionality. Remember, your goal is not to be perfect at each and every one of these practices the first time you try them. That's just not realistic, especially if the information in this chapter is brand-new for you. Your goal is to practice them, and over time, you'll find you're naturally more kind to your spouse or more honest with them.

That doesn't mean you'll respond *only* in positive ways all the time, but it's like working out at the gym—if you keep doing it, you will see amazing results!

CHAPTER 5

Selfishness

Peter

I've been married for almost thirty years, and lately I've reflected on my selfishness levels throughout those three decades.

Early in our relationship, I think I viewed life through a pretty me-centric lens. I tended to focus on my own wants and needs. I grew as we had children, though, because I naturally invested more and more of myself into them. That took most of my focus off myself. In fact, I probably invested in them by denying focusing on my own wants and needs to a fault. But when every day or week feels like there's so much to be done, it's easy to lose sight of the bigger picture and just do what's right in front of you.

What I'm seeing in myself now that all my kids are grown and out of the house surprises me. I don't approach life from a selfless perspective as naturally as I did when they were here. I'm focusing on myself more. I tend to think it's now "my time" to focus on me and on what I want out of life. I'm more particular now, and I tend to be more selfish with my time (I like relaxing evenings and weekends). I'm also more self-centered with my purchases or with what I do, because I feel like I've earned that. I don't come out and say I deserve "me time," but I think my subconscious motivation is that I've earned the right to be selfish because I've been giving and serving for so many years. I want what I want, and I want it now.

This isn't a pattern I've noticed only in myself. I often see this happen as I counsel couples who've become empty nesters. Despite the fact that we would assume people in their late forties or in their fifties or sixties would be mature and generous, lots of couples struggle as a result of their slowly drifting apart because they've each started focusing primarily on themselves. This has been a struggle for me too.

. . . . .

As painful as it may be to admit it, we all have natural tendencies toward selfishness. Most of our ideas and decisions run through a filter before they make it out into the world: *How will this affect me?* For some of us, that's an ugly and hard truth to accept. Others of us already know this is our normal decision-making process, and we see nothing wrong with it. But selfishness damages relationships—especially our marriages.

Alan

We do, however, need to understand what is selfish and what is not. Nobody ever taught me this explicitly, but I grew up thinking it was selfish to ever express my own wants and opinions. So when a group I was in needed to decide where to eat dinner, I always said I was good with whatever everybody else wanted. Then when they decided on Taco Bell, I would be disappointed and feel cheated because I wanted to go to McDonald's. But nobody could have known that because I never gave any input! Hopefully, you can't relate to that approach, but I'm guessing many people can.

. . . . .

We chose to highlight that mind-set because we can all tend to misunderstand the concepts of selfishness and selflessness. We can fail to see the difference. Selflessness doesn't mean not thinking about yourself *at all*; it's the opposite of selfishness, which means thinking of yourself as more important than others. Thinking your plans for the weekend are more important than your spouse's needs and wants. Thinking your stress from work is the only thing the people in your family are dealing with.

You see how easy this is. It even makes sense from a certain perspective, because we do have legitimate needs like spending some time relaxing or decompressing after a stressful situation.

But too often we start thinking the situation we're dealing with is the *only* one that matters. We forget we're not the only person dealing with disappointment, feeling overwhelmed, or needing some time to unwind.

Dan

Unless we actively fight against selfishness in our marriages, it's easy to find ourselves living separate lives from our spouses. I know of a couple who each have such a strong independent streak that they drive separate cars to church on Sunday morning even though they attend the same service. But the husband prefers one route, and the wife prefers the other. There's nothing necessarily wrong with this, but it's hard to imagine that this mentality doesn't seep into their daily conversations. You can see how this couple might start eating separate meals at home because they prefer different foods, sleeping in separate rooms because they prefer different room temperatures, and claiming different areas of the house and garage as their preferred hangout spaces. In short, you can see this mind-set resulting in two people living completely separate lives under the same roof.

Again, if you and your spouse do some of these things, that's not necessarily a huge issue. But if you see yourselves starting to allow selfishness to seep into more significant decisions, that might be a signal that you both need to take a look inward to check for areas of selfishness.

. . . . .

The thing about selfishness is that it's so insidious. Like we mentioned before, it feels completely understandable and justifiable along the way, but if we aren't proactive about surrendering when we notice selfishness in our lives, it's far too easy to end up complaining to friends or family about our spouse and working to get them on our side. And your spouse may be doing the same. Once we start thinking of ourselves first and foremost, we can think we're doing the right thing as we head down this road of self-justification and spouse blaming. But if we're aiming to have a purposeful marriage, we need to remember there's nothing purposeful about that.

We all need to live an others-oriented life. In marriage, that means we think of our spouse as an equally valuable person created in the image of God. We all know that thinking would make our marriages better, but it can still be hard to live it out when we're caught up in the moment, feeling physically or emotionally drained. Those are the moments when we especially get the opportunity to practice selfless behavior.

The Selfishness Cure: Empathy

Peter

In 1999, my wife and I went through an extremely difficult period. Our children were young— always a demanding stage of life for parents—so when Shawn Maree was feeling uncharacteristically depleted, we thought her struggle might be due to our full and busy household. Our youngest, Sophia, had been born only a few months prior, so Shawn was caring for a baby along with our preschooler, Isaak, and our kindergartener, Megan. As the weeks went by, though, she wasn't getting stronger. In fact, she'd become more and more fatigued. Even when she rested during the day after a full night of sleep, she was often worn-out if not exhausted. But Shawn is persistent and doesn't give up, so she continued to push through the difficult days.

After months of that baseline, Shawn felt especially terrible one weekend. We thought she had the flu because she had a fever. The following Monday, while I was at work, she couldn't take it anymore and had her mom come watch the kids so she could go to the ER. She got in touch with me on the way to the hospital and let me know her fever was worsening and she was physically falling apart. She needed help. I met her at the ER, and as the tests continued, the looks between the doctors and nurses grew more concerned and the conversations grew more serious.

Finally the ER doctor said to Shawn, "We're going to transfer you to a larger hospital for more tests and to take the excess fluid off your lungs. You either have a serious case of pneumonia or your body is fighting something else, like cancer."

After many tests and procedures, we came to a whole new reality. Shawn had cancer. We were shocked and completely devastated. We're planners and like to be in control of our lives and circumstances. We create a strategic plan for something, anything, everything. Then we work the plan. It can be about our careers, finances, kids, schedules, or anything else. You name it. No matter the situation, we'll work the plan we came up with. But suddenly the plan—all our plans—just stopped.

As we began to recalibrate life on many levels, we worked hard to settle into the new world we'd just entered. Many aspects of life changed dramatically for us, our marriage, our family, and our jobs. However, it wasn't all bad. This crisis required a major reordering to highlight what was *really* important and what we needed to focus on. But we also identified what we didn't need to worry about and completely pushed it off or forgot about it.

Over the ten months of Shawn's chemotherapy, we still, of course, had to juggle the needs of three little kids, my job, and all the other demands of life. But I also found a cure for selfishness when I developed empathy on a whole new level.

As I sat by Shawn's bedside, I sometimes watched her as she slept. Other times she laid there too exhausted to move yet in too much pain to sleep. I still desired a little love, kindness, and tenderness that only a wife can give a husband, but that was almost impossible as Shawn fought for her life. So, for me, this was also a journey of empathy. A process of growing and learning how to serve and care for my sick spouse. How to love her well and show up for her despite her not being able to do much for me.

Over the course of that yearlong struggle with many ups and downs, I wouldn't say I questioned God and his goodness; I was mostly just exhausted and confused. And through those dark days, we were blessed to have family and friends to lean on like never before. We also saw God more often in daily life and grew closer to him. And we found several Scriptures that spoke truth to us:

> As the heavens are higher than the earth, so are my ways higher than your ways and my thoughts than your thoughts. (Isaiah 55:9)

> Humble yourselves, therefore, under God's mighty hand, that he may lift you up in due time. Cast all your anxiety on him because he cares for you. (1 Peter 5:6–7)

> Do not be anxious about anything, but in every situation, by prayer and petition, with thanksgiving, present your requests to God. And the peace of God, which transcends all understanding, will guard your hearts and your minds in Christ Jesus. (Philippians 4:6–7)

The main verse we adopted was Proverbs 19:21: "Many are the plans in a person's heart, but it is the LORD's purpose that prevails."

I'm blessed to say Shawn made it and is alive and well today. We made it as a couple and a family. I made it individually and learned a tremendous amount about myself, about God, about how to lean on his people, and about empathy. And yet I continue to have so much to learn about how to serve and care for my wife in each new season of our lives and marriage.

Developing Empathy

Empathy is the ability to feel or understand what another person is feeling or going through. And as Peter and Shawn's story illustrates, it's an absolutely vital part of a growing and strong marriage. Difficult times certainly highlight its importance, but empathy is also hugely important in daily life.

If we're honest, though, we have to admit that sometimes the barrier to our being empathetic toward our spouses is the amount of effort it takes. It's much easier to operate from our own perspective. After all, that's what we've been doing for most or all of our lives. Empathy takes intentional effort, and it also takes a surprising amount of emotional energy to practice it. It requires us to put our initial reactions and thoughts on the backburner as we imagine life from our partner's perspective.

That's hard enough to do when things are going well between the two of us, but when conflict, hardship, or trauma is involved, the challenge grows even more intense.

That's when it's helpful to remember a deeper reason to show empathy in the moment: Our spouse is created in the image of God and is immensely valuable to him. Our spouse has a deep physical or emotional need. Life isn't all about us and what we need or want or feel in the moment. Whatever your deeper reason is, remember it when you're tempted to see life *only* through your own lens. When you practice empathy, you will constantly be surprised at just how much your partner's behavior makes sense when you see a situation or issue from their perspective.

Just like any area of life you're trying to grow in, developing these "empathy muscles" will take time. But as you consistently work on seeing things from your spouse's perspective, you'll get better at it over time. It will even start to become more natural. And it will radically transform your relationship with your spouse. It will also transform your perspective of the world.

Empathy for your spouse won't happen without your being intentional about it and working to understand where your partner is coming from, how they feel, and what things feel like from their perspective. Yet empathy will make a huge impact when you're going through a heavy or tough time as a couple. It also brings a lot of healing and peace in moments that have a lot less gravity. Think of how often your conflict is over one or both of you being selfish. Or over each of you having a completely different perspective on something that isn't a massive issue in the big picture.

A Surprising Way Self-Focus Shows Up

Do you think your spouse feels loved, accepted, and understood? This is so foundational to marriage. And as you ask yourself that question, understand that each person is different. Not in the sense that some people don't need those things; everyone does. But in the sense that what makes *you* feel loved, accepted, or understood is sometimes different from what makes your spouse feel loved, accepted, or understood.

Maybe you didn't know this would be the case before you got married, but marriage has been hard at work teaching you this fact. We've all had the experience of saying something we meant to be encouraging, but our spouse didn't find it to be meaningful—or even found it to be demeaning. Or we've said something we meant to point out a fact, but our spouse found it to be humiliating or hurtful. You could probably give several examples of how your well-intentioned words or actions had a different impact on your spouse than you expected. Or maybe they even had the exact opposite effect you intended!

In the moment, it's hard to make this connection, but these experiences teach us that what makes us each feel loved, accepted, and understood is not necessarily what makes our spouse feel that way. When we have such a misunderstanding in real time, we tend to react defensively or in disbelief. *How could you possibly take that the wrong way?* We've all been there, as both the one who misinterprets our spouse and as the one who's been misinterpreted.

Alan

I had a funny realization about this aspect of our relationship in the first year or so of our marriage. I was thinking about Jesus's teaching to "do to others what you would have them do to you" (Matthew 7:12). I had always interpreted that verse literally, so I would be completely direct with people and tell them exactly what I was thinking. I would pretty much praise people only based on their effort, their thoughtfulness, or their going above and beyond expectations. I thought I was being empathetic by basing my responses on how I answered the question, *How would I feel if that happened to me?*

At first glance, that's exactly what Jesus was teaching. But I was consistently running into issues. I never praised people for doing what was expected of them because, to me, that's just the minimum expected. You don't deserve praise for doing the minimum. I would also be direct with people about what I thought, but they would get upset with me. And when that happened, I had a thought that—again, to me—was pretty funny: *Thanks a lot, Jesus. I'm doing exactly what you said, but it keeps blowing up in my face.* I don't know if you ever have confrontational conversations with God, but I do. And as you can imagine, I slowly learned that the fault was actually with me.

Jesus didn't mean you should do to other people the exact thing you want them to do to you. He meant you should do what will communicate to them the same thing you want communicated to you. That's a bit of a nuanced difference, but I hope my personal examples of missing the point help clarify what I mean. In most cases, telling me I did a good job only communicated that the person didn't *expect* me to do a good job. So I would treat Annaliese like she was wired the exact same way I was. Inadvertently, then, I failed to communicate how much I valued my wife in my efforts to communicate value to her!

Do you see how disorienting it can be to try to give your spouse the gift of feeling loved, accepted, and understood when you're wired differently? But I started trying to practice what Jesus really meant with Annaliese. Whenever she did a good job with something, I told her

I was proud of her and that she'd done a good job. I'd realized saying those things communicated value to her.

If you've been approaching marriage like I did, treating your spouse *the exact way* you want to be treated, I hope you can learn from my example and realize that you may have a blind spot. You may be unknowingly self-focused by interpreting so much of life through your own lens instead of your spouse's lens. But as I started communicating love, acceptance, and understanding to Annaliese the way she needed to feel those things to feel valued, I saw the joy she experienced.

To this day, it's still weird for me to say things to her *I* would interpret as demeaning or even offensive, but I've finally learned to be obedient to the spirit of Jesus's teaching and say and do what lets Annaliese know she's indeed loved, accepted, and understood.

I encourage you to ask yourself if you have any blind spots in this area of your marriage. Are you treating your spouse the way *you* want to be treated? Or the way *they* want to be treated?

• • • • •

Gary Chapman's *The 5 Love Languages* is a breakthrough work that has helped many couples find and name their blind spots when it comes to how they are loving their spouses. In the book, he writes about five "love languages" and suggests that each of us are primarily wired to receive love through one of these ways: words of affirmation, acts of service, receiving gifts, quality time, and physical touch.[13]

Lots of people find their primary love language is different from their spouse's. And if you've been missing the mark in this area, we hope our stories have let you know you're not alone. The complexities, however, arise when we try to give and show love primarily through the means we would most need to receive it, regardless of whether that's what our spouse needs.

Peter

I've often tried to show Shawn love by using my own "love language." I assume that any normal person wants affection and touch. So I would be affectionate with her without realizing I was doing that because it's what would communicate love *to me*. Or I would clean and organize things around the house, because if she did that for me, it would communicate just how much she loved and cared about me. I expended lots of effort and expected a big response of gratitude from her. But I was showing her love *my way* instead of *her way*.

The lesson I've had to learn is that Shawn needs quality time with me. That's what communicates my love for her in a way she's wired to receive it. Some of the time we're together can feel like we're just "doing nothing" to me, but even that time together makes Shawn feel loved, accepted, and understood.

• • • • •

If we can make that mental shift—thinking about our interactions with our spouses through the lens of how they're wired and what communicates love, acceptance, and understanding to them—we'll be setting ourselves up for success and loving our spouses well. It takes an extra step or two of effort on our part, but it's worth it when we can learn to speak our spouse's "language" more and more fluently as time goes on. It makes our marriage much more purposeful.

If your spouse feels love, acceptance, and understanding from you, that's not only giving them a gift but letting them know you're rooting out selfishness and self-focus in order to love them well.

CHAPTER 6

Forgiveness

Marriage gives us all plenty of opportunities to practice forgiving. Not because *you* specifically are married to a selfish, difficult person, but because we're people, so we're all selfish and difficult at times. That's part of what it is to be alive. We're all at varying stages of letting go of our need to control, our need for everything to go exactly our way, and our need to do exactly what we want to do exactly when we want to do it. Knowing that marriage is the lifelong joining together of two people who are selfish at least some of the time yet is an invitation for them to build a life together, it's obvious that forgiveness will play a key role in this bond.

A Word on Abuse

Before we get into the "what and why" of forgiveness, let's clarify what forgiveness *isn't*. Too many people have allowed a pattern of physical or emotional abuse to continue in the name of forgiveness. (And that's made even more complicated by Jesus's teaching in Luke 17:4, to forgive somebody seven times in a single day!) If you're being abused, forgiveness doesn't mean you allow the cycle to continue as long as your abuser says the word *sorry* between incidents of abuse.

If that's the situation you find yourself in, seek help! If your physical safety is in jeopardy, get out of the situation! Either way, find a counselor in your area who can work with you. But please do not read this chapter on forgiveness and think it means you need to keep being abused if you want to be faithful to God. You don't.

What Is Forgiveness?

We need to clarify what forgiveness is before we look at some ways it plays out in our relationships. You've probably heard it's important to "forgive and forget," but that advice can be counterproductive when it comes to relationships. If we think forgiveness is tied to our ability to pretend like a hurtful thing never happened, then we'll be slow to forgive our spouse.

Instead of tying forgiveness to forgetting, we need to connect forgiveness to *no longer holding an offense against our spouses.* Think about the difference there. If infidelity has been part of your marriage story, forgiving and forgetting would mean you just pretend like everything is perfectly fine and you have no reason to be cautious in any way the next time your spouse leaves for a business trip or stays late at work. But with a healthy understanding of forgiveness, you can stop holding that offense against your spouse at the same time you put some boundaries in place to prevent that hurtful and destructive behavior from happening again.

Forgiveness is the decision that sets you free from holding on to anger and bitterness against another person. It's a decision that allows you to stop living in the past and start working to create a better present and future. With that perspective on forgiveness, do you see how things can change?

Forgiveness is a vital part of growing and healing a marriage. It's crucial to have a heart that forgives if we're going to have a purposeful marriage. When we refuse to forgive, we get stuck in the past. Wounds from years ago continue to color our responses to our spouse if we don't make the decision to forgive, but forgiveness allows us to stay in the present and move into the future. Without that ability, we get stuck in the past. Holding on to unforgiveness locks hurt and anger in place like nothing else.

Think about how long we can nurse a phrase said to us, an action done to us, or another person's choice that negatively impacted us. We can all probably think of something that happened five or more years ago and still feel some of those feelings right now. That's the insidious nature of refusing to forgive. We can continue to replay the old tapes of how we've been hurt, disappointed, misunderstood, or abused. And when we replay the tapes, we can be transported right back to that moment and feel the (probably justified) anger and bitterness that hurtful situation warranted.

But mentally going back in time doesn't do us any good. Henry Cloud and John Townsend have this to say about forgiveness in *Boundaries*: "To forgive means we will never get from that person what was owed us. And that is what we do not like, because that involves grieving for what will never be: The past will not be different."[14] That is so beautifully and powerfully stated. No matter how much we wish it were true and no matter how much it's fair for us to wish it, the past will not be different. When we choose to forgive, we make peace with that fact. This chapter focuses on how we can do that.

As we take a look at what forgiveness is, it will be obvious that it will have a huge impact on your marriage. But you will also benefit from practicing forgiveness in all your relationships. With that in mind, we'll lay out a few aspects of forgiveness that are not exclusive to marriage but will make a huge difference when you put them into practice in all your other relationships.

Peter

I wrote a lot about forgiveness in my book *Winning the Battle Over Abuse*, and I want to share five points that were part of a Forgiveness Worksheet in that book, several of which reinforce what you've already read. I'll include a couple of quotes below along with some new perspectives and explanations for each point.

1. Forgiveness is a choice.

Letting go of resentment and thoughts of revenge is an act of the will. It's also a process, especially when the offense was exceptionally painful. But when you choose not to forgive, you are the one who suffers the most. It's hard to believe, but when you're holding on to hurt, anger, and bitterness, forgiveness actually allows you to experience the full abundance of life God has for you. Once you choose to forgive, he begins to set your heart free from anger, hurt, and pain, and Satan loses his power to work.

Please don't read these words and think you're doing something wrong if forgiving isn't as easy as snapping your fingers and choosing to move past the hurt. In this process, your emotions often won't match intellectual decisions, especially at first. But stick with it. It will be hard work, but it's worth it. The reality is writing and reading about forgiveness is a lot easier than living it out.

2. Forgiveness is **not** *the same as forgetting.*

As we mentioned at the beginning of this chapter, forgetting is often considered part of forgiveness. That's an idea we've all heard and many of us have been taught. But that's not quite the reality of the situation. Forgetting about an offense may be a result of forgiving, but it's never the means to that end. You don't make hurt, anger, or bitterness go away by pretending they don't exist in the first place.

From *Winning the Battle Over Abuse*:

> You are going to live with the consequences of evil whether you want to or not, but it's your choice to do it in bitterness and pain of unforgiveness or to live in the freedom of forgiveness. It does not mean that you tolerate the sin that was committed against you. Remembering what happened allows you to learn and grow from your experience.[15]

Forgiving others, whether it's our spouse or somebody else who's hurt us, allows us to let go of the past and move into the future. If we don't make that choice, we'll find that we bring our baggage, our triggers, and our trauma with us until we do.

3. Forgiveness is not about the other person deserving it.

In the Lord's Prayer, Jesus teaches his disciples to pray, "Forgive us our debts as we also have forgiven our debtors" (Matthew 6:12). Jesus teaches us to ask for God's forgiveness in the same breath we talk about the forgiveness we've offered others. Old Testament professor Donald Gowan adds this: "Human forgiveness must be an important subject for the New Testament, for it appears in the Lord's Prayer, the only human activity that Jesus included in the Prayer."[16]

Then after Jesus finishes the rest of the prayer, he says, "If you forgive other people when they sin against you, your heavenly Father will also forgive you. But if you do not forgive others their sins, your Father will not forgive your sins" (verses 14–15). He doesn't say anything about the sorrow of the person who wronged you, or their commitment to stop doing it, or anything else. This statement from Jesus helps us see just how seriously God takes forgiveness and how he expects us to emulate him in this area. On the cross, Jesus said, "Father, forgive them, for they do not know what they are doing" (Luke 23:34). He didn't just teach the importance of forgiveness; he lived it!

That kind of attitude is the *last* thing we naturally feel in a moment when we've been slighted, offended, let down, or worse. But it's what Jesus chose in a moment of immense pain, betrayal, and disappointment. You can see that, when he talks about forgiveness, he has the ultimate credibility.

When we remember that God forgives us when we don't deserve it, we see just how high a calling it is to forgive others the way God forgives us. We are called to forgive out of our love for and obedience to Christ. We also forgive so we can be free from our bonds to the past.

4. Forgiveness is difficult.

This is so obvious that it almost feels like it could go unsaid. But that would be doing us all a disservice. It's important to be reminded that if we're struggling to forgive, we're not alone. Like anything else we do that's difficult, we will make mistakes and missteps along the way. We'll find ourselves nurturing bitterness and anger rather than surrendering them to God. We'll find ourselves recoiling when we think of or see the person who hurt us so deeply.

It's normal to feel pain and hurt, but the way we react to that pain and hurt is often unhealthy and not what God calls us to. We can find ourselves trying to be the one to judge our offenders and punish them for their behavior. And, as pastor Pierre Eade says so well in his book *Our Good Father*, we can try to "hand them over to God" and pretend that we forgave:

> At times we can muster up the ability to forgive others, but we still want them to be on the hook with God. We forgive, but we hope, expect and may even ask for God to judge. "I forgive them, Lord. Now you go after them." If we examined our hearts, we would realize that, at times, we actually hope for a worse outcome for the people we "forgive" by placing people into God's hands! We forgive them, but hope God will judge them! Until you forgive the person who has caused you hurt and pain, you allow them to control your thoughts, emotions, and actions.[17]

Again, that doesn't mean you leave yourself just as vulnerable to being hurt again, and it also doesn't mean that trust is immediately restored.

5. Don't wait to forgive until you feel like forgiving, because you will never get there!

It's nearly impossible to *feel* like forgiving when we've been hurt, and waiting for that feeling will leave you stuck in anger and bitterness. Instead, start the process regardless of how you feel. I promise, it will be worth it.

From *Winning the Battle Over Abuse*:

> Forgiveness is often a slow process. It requires a daily, sometimes hourly, decision. It may require a lifetime of forgiving, but it is important to the Lord. Your feelings will take time to heal, but in giving the gift of forgiveness to others, you also receive a gift—freedom in Christ.[18]

Alan

Although I won't go into the background of this experience, I think many of you will be able to relate to it on some level. I was deeply wronged, and I was angry. This person's face would flash into my mind at random times, and I would fixate on how they had hurt and wronged me. On how I was right to be hurt and how unfair it was. If I explained the full situation, you would agree that I was justifiably angry. I had been the innocent victim.

The weeks of anger and bitterness turned into months of it—anytime this person's face flashed in my mind. Then in a moment of honesty, I realized I hated this person. That scared me as I thought of Jesus's teachings on avoiding hate and choosing love (Matthew 5). I also thought of 1 John 2:9: "Anyone who claims to be in the light but hates a brother or sister is still in the darkness." On an intellectual level, I knew this hate was wrong, but that's how I felt. And even worse, I felt completely justified. I was fully aware that this hatred didn't match up with messages I was preaching at churches about God's grace and compassion, but I still felt hatred toward this person.

I had two pretty obvious issues. First, I didn't *want* to forgive them. And second, I didn't even want to *want* to forgive them. Do you see the distinction there? I was so convinced that I was justified to feel the way I did that I wasn't even open to forgiveness.

So I started asking God to help me reach a point where I was at least *open* to working toward forgiving this person. That process wasn't short or simple. I spent multiple weeks praying about it. Eventually my heart started to soften, and I realized I was finally open to working toward forgiveness. I actually wanted to do the right thing and forgive this person. But I still wasn't there yet. So

I spent lots more time asking God to keep softening my heart—this time to work on actually forgiving. And again, this wasn't a matter of days but weeks.

As I continued to pray and time continued to pass, the anger and bitterness started to fade. And now I don't hate this person. I don't hope bad things happen to them. I doubt we'll ever be best friends, but with God's help, I've let go of the anger and hatred I had toward them.

I'm telling this story because I don't want you to read about forgiveness and feel like something is wrong with you if it takes a long time, a lot of work, and a lot of prayer and surrender to get there. Sometimes forgiving will even seem nearly impossible. But forgiveness is a process, and that's okay!

Moving On

Sometimes people ask themselves, *Have I really forgiven if I'm still angry?* That's a great and important question. Like we've mentioned throughout this chapter, forgiveness is a choice we need to keep making and a process we need to keep going through. It's both a "moment in time" event when we choose to forgive and an ongoing process that we may have to continually choose to live in moment by moment. It's possible that our anger and bitterness will flash back up when we see the person who hurt us or when we think about what they did. But that's a good time to choose to continue to forgive.

As we were working on this chapter, we talked about the complexity of forgiveness being both a one-time decision and a continual process. We thought about how walking with God is similar in a lot of ways. In a single moment, we decide to give our lives to him, and then we spend months and years and decades living out that decision. We don't do it perfectly, but we're constantly having to choose surrender and to make him Lord instead of ourselves. In the same way, forgiveness is a singular-moment decision and a constantly-lived-out-over-years commitment.

Letting Go of the Little Stuff

We close this chapter on a bit of a lighter note by talking about forgiving things in our marriages that are much more in the category of annoyances, inconveniences, or just different preferences—the little stuff.

Dan

It may seem strange, but for a period of time I kept a running list of everything Jane and I disagreed about. Not to "build my case" against her but to recognize some of the ridiculous conflicts we allow to escalate in the daily flow of life. This is my complete list of what Jane and I disagreed about:

- The fact that the neighbor's dog used the bathroom in our yard
- The children
- Simply White Toothpaste
- The way she thinks
- The children
- Using the recycling bin
- The way I think
- A step I accidentally missed (this is not a metaphor...I'm talking about a stair step)
- The children
- A big orange construction barrel from the highway that ended up in our house
- The way she broke her fingernail
- A big orange construction barrel from the highway that ended up in our house (yes, this was a second conflict over that)

I hope my list gave you a good laugh! But I also hope you see how normal your relationship is if you have conflict about things that would be embarrassing to share with anybody else. In light of that, we all need to ask ourselves how we can ensure we absolutely refuse to get hung up on stuff that doesn't matter.

• • • • •

One of the best ways to help us do that is by taking this advice from British philosopher A. C. Grayling:

> When we cease laying blame we either take responsibility for our own contribution, or become free to recognize that blame is irrelevant...and laying blame is a waste of energy which could be better directed at repairing damage or starting afresh.[19]

Getting away from the blame game in our relationships is key to letting go of the little stuff—the stuff that doesn't ultimately matter and that we would be embarrassed to admit we had conflict over. Keeping the big picture in mind is helpful in those moments. Ask yourself, *Will this matter in five years?* Most of the time, the honest answer is that you probably won't even *remember* it in five years. Taking the long view and remembering that you and your spouse are committed to being on the same team rather than being against each other will make a big difference in those moments. And it will allow you to let go of things you may otherwise find yourself holding on to longer than you should.

CHAPTER 7

Apologizing

Right after reading about forgiveness, it's time to cover another tough component of marriage and relationships—apologizing. Just like we do when it comes to offering forgiveness, we can go into defensive mode when it's time to apologize. Maybe we think, *Well, I wouldn't have done what I did if she hadn't done what she did.* Or *He never apologizes when he messes up, so I'm not going to apologize either.*

Those examples of justifications are a little more on the nose than the ones we can actually use to convince ourselves, though. It's much easier to think about, for instance, all the stress we've been dealing with at work and be annoyed that our spouse added to that stress by bringing up an issue when they knew we were already overwhelmed. Or to think about how it doesn't make sense to apologize because the point we made was right!

Sadly, these examples were easy to come up with. And just knowing how and when to apologize doesn't make it easy to put it into practice all the time. So if you noticed this chapter is about apologizing and found yourself groaning a little bit, tempted to skip to chapter 8, know that you're not alone!

Even though it's not an easy journey, learning how to genuinely apologize and then actually doing it is yet another key to a great relationship. But in many ways, the ability and willingness to offer a genuine apology is becoming a lost art. In his counseling work, Peter has seen many people's marriages improve dramatically as they started practicing apologizing on a regular basis. Time and time again, he's been witness to what a huge help for struggling couples it can be.

Scripture uses the concept of *repentance*, which is familiar to you if you've spent much time in church. But, interestingly, repentance isn't often explained very well. The way it's normally used, we assume it just means something like *Admit you're a total failure and stop doing bad things*. So when John the Baptist is preparing the way for Jesus and calls out, "The kingdom of God has come near. Repent and believe the good news!" in Mark 1:15, we can read repentance as a shameful kind of thing. *The kingdom is here, so stop being so awful and come be better.* In that context, it's not quite a stirring or inviting offer.

A better way to define *repent* is to change your mind, turn around, or course correct. John, and later Jesus, isn't saying you're doing bad stuff and you need to stop. He's saying you're living the wrong way but you can change course. You can change your mind and do things God's way—the best way!

That's the same attitude we need to have with our spouses. If we see admitting we were wrong and apologizing as weakening or diminishing our "position," then we have the completely wrong approach. We do need to admit we were wrong and apologize, but the reason behind that isn't so our spouse can rub our faces in it, just like we don't admit we were wrong and apologize to God so he can rub our faces in it. We do it so we can be made right—both with God and with our spouse.

Like we've done with other familiar concepts in this book, we'll break down what an apology looks like when you make a mistake that has hurt your spouse—in seven steps:

1. Admit what you did.

It doesn't matter whether the hurt you caused your spouse was intentional or accidental. Either way, you need to apologize. Often, when the hurt is unintentional, it may feel unfair to be asked to apologize. This is pretty odd, because if you stepped on your spouse's foot or accidentally bumped into them, causing them to stumble, it would be completely natural to apologize. But when the mistake or the hurt is emotional rather than physical, it can be tempting to skip this step. Don't. Admitting what you did requires a lot of humility and vulnerability—both of which are hard to live out—but the amazing thing is that those difficult choices ultimately lead to a deeper relationship with your spouse.

2. Check your body language and tone.

This isn't necessarily Step 2; it's more a Part B that applies to each of the steps of an apology. Think about how many meanings you can give to these two words, depending on body language and tone: "Yeah. Great." You could communicate that you're excited, committed, sarcastic, dismissive, or a number of other things. All during an apology (and in conversations in general), it's important to communicate sincerity and care through not just our words but our tone and body language.

3. Genuinely apologize.

It might strike you as weird that we've made the apology itself the *third* step in this process, but seeing it in the flow of all the other steps should help that make sense.

A true apology sincerely expresses our sorrow for our words or actions that caused someone pain or difficulty. And once we acknowledge our mistake and adopt the right tone and body language, an apology makes sense and is believable.

If genuinely apologizing is new for you, or if you never saw it modeled growing up, let us give you three ways you could begin:

> "I'm sorry. . ."
> "I apologize for. . ."
> "I regret that I. . ."

Do *not* start a sentence with one of these phrases and then say "but" and explain all the ways your spouse "caused" you to do what you did. A genuine apology is focused on what you did or said that wasn't right. There *is* a time and a place for going back and talking about what led up to the conflict, but this isn't it! An apology does not require an explanation or justification. The point is to acknowledge that you did something that hurt your spouse. Keep it short and keep it sincere. When it comes to apologizing, less is often more.

4. Do something different next time.

As mentioned in Step 3, an apology sincerely expresses your sorrow, which means an apology isn't really an apology unless you experience a change in your heart. Your motives have to change, and your actions should too! Again, we see a parallel with repentance. Our mind and our course should change as a result, and that means trying hard not to make the same mistake in the future.

5. Determine what went wrong.

Alan

Annaliese and I often use what I call a Conflict Postmortem, a separate part of the conversation that takes place *after* an apology. Maybe Conflict Postmortem seems like a grim name for this practice, but just like a physical postmortem looks at a body and works backward to determine the cause of death, a Conflict Postmortem looks at the moment of conflict and works backward to determine what went wrong. It's been a helpful tool for us as we work to deescalate conflict and avoid having the same issue over and over as we move forward.

Here's how I described the Conflict Postmortem in *Marriage: Five Years Later*:

> The conversation begins with a genuine apology from one or both of us and leads to us talking about how the conflict started. The point of this part of the conversation isn't to find excuses or justifications but to look back on the conflict and its escalation to figure out what exactly went on. We look at how the situation and our reactions played into what happened, what happened, why it happened, how we felt as it was happening, and how we can avoid a similar situation in the future.[20]

This is about fact-finding in a non-judgmental way so both people feel safe sharing their perspective. But again, the absolute most important thing about using this approach is being clear that you're moving from the "apology" part of a conversation to the Conflict Postmortem part. If that's not clear, digging into what happened and how it happened may make your spouse feel like you're evading responsibility, being defensive, and refusing to admit you were wrong and apologize.

6. Keep the goal in mind.

The ultimate goal of addressing any conflict is to determine how the two of you can move forward as a team. If a conversation about an apology ends with one party feeling beat down and discouraged, you're missing the mark. And if it ends with one party feeling elevated and faultless, you're missing the mark. Apologies exist so the offending party can admit their mistake, ask for forgiveness, and commit to doing better next time. They exist so the offended party can be recognized and validated. When either person walks away from an apology feeling less peaceful or more singled out, it's time to have an apology about the apology! The goal is to walk away reminded that you're on the same team. It's not the two of you against each other; it's the two of you together against any obstacle you face.

*7. **Live it out.***

It's possible that some of the six steps above are quite different from what you've seen modeled by the people in your life. Whether with parents, grandparents, bosses, teachers, or some other influential person in your life, it's likely that you've seen "apologies" that didn't involve admitting or changing anything. Even if that's the case, now it's your turn to be a great example. Your marriage and any other people around you will benefit as you practice the discipline of apologizing well. It will make an impact both inside and outside your home.

Especially if genuinely apologizing is new for you, know that practice will make it easier, more comfortable, and more natural. It's weird at first. It's awkward and hard. But keep doing it, because it's the right thing to do.

You'll also realize that holding back an apology is often an attempt to protect something you don't need to protect. In other words, failing to apologize doesn't make other people think you haven't made a mistake in the first place. In most cases, everyone who was there knows you made a mistake, and by refusing to acknowledge it and apologize, you're almost choosing to "double down" on the wrong thing you did.

Apologizing is also a great way to learn and practice humility and surrender. Humble people admit their mistakes, apologize, and then change. And genuinely apologizing and learning to do it well will absolutely improve all our horizontal relationships. But it also honors God and draws us closer to him. Let's all strive to be those kinds of people—especially in our marriages.

CHAPTER 8

Differences

Problems aren't caused by differences. They're caused by not handling differences well. With that in mind, then, we need healthy ways to handle the frustrations that arise from our differences in marriage. *Everyone* is married to someone with different perspectives than theirs, so even if you and your spouse are similar, the two of you just aren't on the same page in every area.

Here are a few examples that represent the differences we see in our three marriages:

Dan

- Jane is quiet. I'm loud and boisterous.
- She drives 5 MPH under the speed limit. I drive 5 MPH (or more) over it.
- She loves curling up with a good book. I love being on the go and active.

Peter

- Shawn likes quiet and slow mornings. I like to get going right away early in the morning.
- She cranks up the volume with music and the TV. I prefer a quieter home.
- She loves warm weather (and a warmer house). I prefer cooler weather.

Alan

- Annaliese likes decorations and knickknacks. I prefer our living space to be clutter free.
- She fills the gas tank when it's still half full. I wait until the fuel light comes on to even think about filling the tank.
- She loves to be out and about with people. I'm a homebody.

You may have just read one or two examples that echo some of the differences between you and your spouse. It's funny to see them written out so simply, because none of those differences seem "worth" having conflict over, objectively speaking. The trouble is we don't always remain objective when we're living through moments that highlight our differences. We've all had disproportionately heated arguments over driving habits, schedules, household preferences, or something else equally as unimportant in the big picture.

But as we said, problems are not caused *by* our differences; they're caused by handling our differences badly. There *is* a helpful way to address your frustration with your partner's driving habits. Or their level of cleanliness. Or the comment they made while you were out for dinner with another couple. But for some reason, less helpful approaches seem to be the ones that pop into our heads more naturally, don't they? We lapse into bad communication habits we've developed over the years, stemming from negative family-of-origin patterns or personality or character flaws.

But if, for instance, your spouse's aggressive driving habits frustrate you, you can address that with a careful and thoughtful approach. You can say you just want to make sure they're being safe when they drive, even though you know they will continue to drive more aggressively than you do. (By the way, this conversation is best to have while you're not in the car driving somewhere.) It's also important to remember that the journey of marriage is about growing in accepting our spouse instead of changing them, which is too often our goal when expressing a frustration.

If your spouse's cleanliness or house-decorating habits frustrate you, you can take a careful and thoughtful approach there too. You can talk about how when your home environment has a certain feel to it, you feel more peaceful there. Then if your spouse is on a totally different page about that, you can have a conversation and work toward a compromise. Remember, this isn't about how to make differences go away but how to handle them in a way that makes you both feel valued, heard, and understood. We will definitely run into issues when our goal is to get our way rather than to achieve the most harmony we possibly can.

Think about the 90/10 Rule during these conversations. Where is your preference blinding you to the pettiness or "tunnel-vision-ness" of your point? Learn to let go of the stuff that doesn't matter and the stuff that's simply personal preference. This is obviously easier said than done, but most of what we'd like to change about what our spouse does isn't "wrong"; it's just different.

Dan

For Jane and me, the driving difference between us has been mostly handled by Jane: she closes her eyes whenever she feels like I'm driving too aggressively for her comfort. That may strike you as a bizarre "solution," but differences like the ones we highlighted earlier don't have a "right" and a "wrong" approach. Of course, each person feels like they're right and their spouse is wrong, but that's not the reality.

Peter

Handling our morning differences looked like me asking Shawn in a calm, kind tone why she liked slower, quieter mornings and why they were so important to her. Then I explained that I'm much more productive in the morning, so I like to get going and be industrious. We determined that less talk yet more doing is best for our marriage as we start each morning.

Alan

For Annaliese and me, the home decoration differences have been mostly handled with some rooms in the house having a more "minimalist" décor. Again, this is a pretty simple compromise, but differences become big issues when neither of us is willing to compromise and allow our preferences to take a backseat, even for a moment.

Irreconcilable Differences—Again

Remember how, in chapter 1, we said too many people want to use the tough aspects of their marriages as an "out," calling them "irreconcilable differences"? We usually hear that phrase in the context of divorce, but anytime we refuse to compromise and desperately hold on to our need to have our preference acknowledged as "right," that's an irreconcilable difference right there.

In those moments, our only way forward in a purposeful marriage is through compromise. And compromise must happen from both sides consistently. Otherwise it isn't compromise; it's just one person pushing harder for their agenda and refusing to give up until they get their way.

You probably find it odd to see us writing about irreconcilable differences in a book about *improving* your marriage! And although this might surprise you, each of our marriages have a number of things we and our wives just can't get on the same page about. But we want to make this clear: running into many of the issues represented by the phrase *irreconcilable differences* is actually completely normal.

Peter

I often tell couples that every marriage has three to five irreconcilable differences. These are things you will never, ever be on the same page about. Shawn is always going to be more cautious than I am. I will always be blunter or maybe even harsh with our kids while she'll be more lenient with them. Those are two examples of things that really come down to our natural wiring and philosophies on life.

We haven't been able to get on the same page about those things over the course of thirty years of marriage. Shawn always was, and always will be, more cautious and risk-averse than I will be. And as strange as it may seem, knowing that has been helpful for us! It means we don't think we're just *one more conversation* away from saying the thing that will finally help the other person start to think more like we do. It also means we aren't doomed to a disastrous relationship just because we have a few areas where we can't see eye to eye. Differences don't consign you to a future of hating your life. This is about understanding that there are just some issues where you'll never get on the same page.

Alan

To illustrate how knowing to expect a few irreconcilable differences is actually encouraging, I want to share a story from my honeymoon. As I write this, Annaliese and I have been married for around seven years, so you'd think I'd remember all the details of this event perfectly. But I don't. I just remember we ran into some kind of disagreement on our drive back to the condo where we were staying. We each shared our frustrations and our perspectives, then sat in the parking lot and talked for another twenty to thirty minutes. But we just couldn't see a path to compromise.

Annaliese is very much wired to want any conflict to end in closure, which means having a plan for the next time we run into the same situation. But in this case, we realized that the next time we were in the same circumstances, I would still have my perspective and she would still have hers, and they didn't line up. She said something along the lines of, "Well, then I don't know what to do, because we just aren't finding a solution here." In that moment, I vaguely remembered something I'd heard secondhand about Peter's thoughts on irreconcilable differences. I shared that with Annaliese, and it brought us both some comfort. Even though we had reached an impasse, we knew it wasn't uncommon for couples to have that experience.

The fact that neither of us remember what that conflict was about tells you it probably wasn't that big of a deal in the long run. Yet it was our first "un-navigate-able" situation as a married couple, so it felt pretty huge in the moment. But again, just knowing that we should expect to have some irreconcilable differences—with totally different approaches and philosophies—brought us a lot of relief that day.

• • • • •

We completely understand differences even bigger than the ones we've mentioned so far exist. Some of you find yourself in a relationship where you don't agree on religious beliefs. Or on sexual desires and frequency. Or on significant money issues. Or on whether to have kids. Or on whether it's worth moving cross country for a job opportunity or to be closer to family. As the stakes of a decision rise higher and higher, the need for grace, kindness, and clear communication continues to rise as well.

If you're running into differences in some of these major areas, we encourage you to see a marriage counselor or coach. Seeing someone is not a quick fix, and it's not a place to get "answers" as much as a place to improve communication and learn more about how your reactions in the moment can either bring you closer to your goals or push you further from them. If you're open to counseling or coaching, we encourage you to give Winning At Home a call at 616-772-1733 so we can connect you to a counselor or coach. Even if you don't live in an area where we have an office, we'll help you find a service provider in your area.

Our hope is that every couple can learn and use the tools available to make their marriages thrive. For some of you, that does mean seeing a counselor or coach, either as a couple or an individual. For others of you, it means choosing kindness and compromise instead of holding on to the need to be right. Living like that requires sacrifice and surrender, both difficult to choose in the moment. But in the long run, making those healthy choices brings so much hope and healing to the areas in our marriages where, before, we could see only differences and disagreements.

You can also gain wisdom from other people's experiences. Find a mentor couple or individual whose marriage you respect and is willing to help guide you, giving you input and advice on managing some of your challenges. Or you can join a small group with other married couples, or read books or devotionals together as a couple and discuss the ideas in them.

Remember, the problems in marriage aren't caused by our differences. They're caused by handling our differences badly. Yes, it's hard to control our temper or desire to react in the moment. But when we do, we find our differences are much less a point of focus than our similarities and areas of agreement. That makes our marriages and homes much more peaceful.

CHAPTER 9

Staying Connected

We've touched on a few ways married couples start to drift apart, so in this chapter we'll cover three ways you and your spouse can stay connected. By now you've realized marriage on purpose requires intentional action, not passivity, so let's get to it.

Spend Time Together

Peter

As I think about what's taken place in my marriage over the years and talk to people in my role as a therapist, I find myself coming back to the basics—some of the things I've been talking about and trying to live out myself for many years now. For instance, one thing that makes a marriage thrive is the simple practice of spending time together. Remember, I discovered my wife feels loved when she gets quality time with me, and that's made all the difference in our relationship. Yet Shawn and I have still struggled with this.

She and I are both high-energy, type-A people, and our struggle was that our calendars continually filled up so much that we would genuinely be too busy to spend quality time together. But then we found making Sunday a day that's intentionally "our day" helpful. We go to church together on Sunday morning, and then we work hard at not scheduling other activities for the remainder of the day. Shawn and I might go out together, or we might just spend the day at home. We also try to be together an evening or two during the week, but making Sunday our baseline minimum has been hugely important to ensure that we're being intentional about spending time with each other.

Maybe you're a homebody who gets so caught up in a hobby or project that time slips away without being intentional about spending time with your spouse. The one great way Shawn and I spend time together is through joint interests. We both love to hike and walk and bike together because we both enjoy being on the go and active. We also love traveling and seeing new parts of our country and the world together.

. . . . .

Maybe none of those activities sound like a great fit for you and your spouse, but that's okay! The point is that you find *your* thing. Consistent time together, especially doing things you both enjoy, will help keep you from drifting apart.

You might be thinking advising you to spend time together is a little bit too basic to make up a meaningful chunk of a chapter in a book about marriage. But it's such a foundational component of building a strong relationship. Think about what we do with anything we value.

We follow our favorite sports team or player by watching as many of their games as possible, reading up on the team or injury news between games, and following ESPN to get up-to-the-minute opinions on how they're looking moving forward. We work constantly to perfect techniques related to our hobbies and watch YouTube videos or listen to podcasts to learn about new approaches. The only way to learn about something or to stay up-to-date is to devote time and energy to it. We don't improve the skills we use in our jobs without time and energy. If you stopped following any news about your favorite team for a few weeks, you would be completely out of the loop on what happened during that timeframe, and you would feel lost if you got into a conversation about recent events.

The same is true of our relationships. We can't just "take time off" from investing in our partner and expect everything to stay exactly like it was when we *were* devoting time and effort to the relationship. That's why time together is so key. It shows that we value our spouse and want to be updated and in the loop on what's going on in their lives. That we want to know about the ups and downs of their day. Giving our time, attention, and energy are tangible ways we communicate love to our spouses—especially in our increasingly distracted and distractible world.

If you're not spending as much time together as you should be, take steps to correct that. You can start small by committing to going out on a date every other week. As previously mentioned, "dates" can look a lot of different ways. Maybe you go out for dinner and a movie. But maybe going for a hike or playing a round of golf is more in line with your interests. Maybe going to your local arcade and buying $20 worth of tokens to play shoot 'em up games together fits you more as a couple. It's not about *how* you spend time connecting and enjoying each other, and it's not about whether you spend money or don't. It's that you *do* spend time connecting and enjoying each other!

Alan

One of my cousins posts photos of outings with his kids on Facebook and captions them *It only takes a moment to make a moment.* We might think that's cute or cheesy and move on. But think about how many of the most special and memorable moments you've shared with your spouse would otherwise be considered insignificant. Think about your own personal highlight reel for your relationship. For Annaliese and me, memories on our highlight reel include laughing hysterically at some inside joke nobody else would think was funny, going for walks when we engaged in far deeper conversations than expected, shopping for a terrible Christmas ornament each year, and Annaliese finding oddball pictures and stories online to help keep me awake while we drove down to Florida for vacation straight through the night.

Of course, our highlight reel has lots of significant moments on it too. But I mention these simple, seemingly unimportant moments as a reminder. In these "throwaway" times, we could easily miss out on creating some of those memories if we both just defaulted to looking at our screens and not paying attention to each other.

• • • • •

You can probably relate to one of the perspectives we shared here, and the important takeaway is that you do something about it. Come up with a plan to be more intentional about spending time with your spouse.

Maybe putting something down on the calendar is the only way you can ensure a date or quality time will happen. Or maybe you prefer to be more spontaneous and putting something down on the calendar feels a little bit like you're scheduling your spouse for an appointment, which feels too methodical. Whatever it takes to actually make sure you spend time together is the approach you should take.

But if you're not intentional about spending time together—however the planning or the execution looks for you as a couple—you'll find that days and weeks have a way of getting away from you. Urgent work, family, and life responsibilities can keep you busy with no real breaks for a long time. Don't let them. Make sure you spend some quality, intentional time with your spouse to strengthen your bond and remind you both of how much you enjoy each other.

Quality time together is different from just being in the same room watching Netflix or even planning the logistics of schedules with kids. Quality time is intentionally choosing to enjoy each other, and one aspect of that is not just recovering from the last busy season but setting goals together, discussing significant areas in your relationship.

Set Goals Together

The tricky thing about these conversations is that you have to be in a healthy place to have them. A lot of times, we launch into a conversation about working on our relationship but it goes poorly because we're worn-out and exhausted from jobs or a number of events and activities. Our guess is that you've had a similar experience in your own relationship—especially if one person is more passionate about the topic than the other.

The key is to be intentional about setting aside time for these talks and both of you knowing what the conversation will be about. If you resist that idea because it sounds like you're setting up a business meeting with your spouse, then use different language. Call it your Friday Update or a Get on the Same Page conversation. The point isn't what you call it, or even the solemnity of the conversation, but rather that you spend time talking about what might not come up in conversation naturally. Talking about what's going on in your relationship, about your finances, about how to invest in your kids (whether they're young or adults), or maybe just about your dreams for the future—and then about your goals in that area.

Goals look different for every couple. Your primary goals might be in the realm of family and raising kids. Or of building a business. Or about creating an income stream so you can volunteer more of your time or donate more money to a cause you both care about deeply. The goals might be as straightforward as getting together once a year to talk about what the coming months look like and strategize how you can stay close as a couple, stay emotionally connected, grow in a specific aspect of your relationship, or weather the storm of a particularly grueling season of life.

Without connecting about these things on purpose, we have a tendency to drift apart as we both slowly start to live in our own heads and come up with our own plans and solutions for what actually impacts both of us. So both time together and this kind of quality time are necessary to avoid that drift in your relationship. And this doesn't just apply to newlyweds or busy couples in the middle of life. It also applies to empty nesters or retirees. All couples need to spend meaningful time together and set goals.

Tap into Your Marriage Reserve Tank

Dan

Some days in marriage—or lots of days—are good and smooth. Some days no conflict comes up and your perspectives just align. But that's not always the case.

I've been married to Jane for about fourteen thousand days. Think about it. After that many days together, anyone would get on your nerves. It just happens. How many days do you think you could spend six to eight hours with somebody without experiencing conflict? If you picture a coworker, you've probably had conflict with many of them. If you picture a best friend, that's not a conflict-free relationship either. But when it comes to marriage, when we face conflict, disappointment, and frustration, we can find ourselves reaching what feels like the end of our rope.

When Jane and I first started this fourteen-thousand-day journey of marriage, I wasn't a pastor, a speaker, or an author. I was the head of accounting for a hospital. I studied accounting in college, and that was my initial career field before I changed careers, feeling like I was supposed to go into ministry. I tell you that background because it makes it even stranger that, early in our marriage, I decided to keep track of the times I thought I'd made a mistake marrying Jane.

Maybe you find that surprising, or at least surprising that I'm willing to share that with you. But I'm an open book about struggles, because I think part of the reason God led me to work with families was so my life can serve as an example of what real family life and real marriage looks like. Jane and I certainly don't do either perfectly! But I've learned some great lessons along the way. And at one year, three years, seven years, and eleven years in our marriage, I did have that thought—that I'd made a mistake marrying Jane. That I didn't feel connected to her anymore. That I wasn't sure we were going to make it.

Interestingly, on the other side of those moments, our marriage was consistently stronger than before. In those tough times, rely on your reserve tank filled with memories of better times. At around year one, I thought back on what it was like when we were dating and engaged. And around year three, I thought about the highlights of our life together over those previous years.

I'm guessing most of you know exactly what I'm talking about. You've thought *I don't know if we're going to get through this and stay married.* But from experience, I can tell you that sticking with it and thinking back on your history together—going back to your marriage reserve tank—is helpful in those difficult times.

Peter

Part of our marriage reserve tank is in the form of Shawn and me keeping a record of our good memories—a "blessings journal." We jot notes in our Bibles or devotionals to highlight and remember our best and most beautiful days. You could also save these memories by taking photos or videos. Documenting the special times as they're happening gives you the opportunity to look back on them when you go through a more painful period in your marriage.

. . . . .

If you can think back on the good days and weeks and years you've shared together, you'll find a lot of strength and perseverance to keep going through the tough times. Even if you think all will be well, be prepared. Tough times will eventually come. They might be the result of words or actions from one of you. Or something totally outside of your control. It could be anything—a wayward child, the loss of a son or daughter, financial insecurity, sexual disconnect, extreme busyness, or any number of other legitimately challenging things.

In those times you'll feel like your marriage is running on fumes. Tap into your memories of overcoming difficulties together in the past and how God has shown up in your life together over the years.

No matter what brings us to questioning whether our marriage will make it, perseverance is key. The popular word to describe perseverance today is *grit.* And grit is a big part of a great marriage. A bond between a couple can gain a surprising amount of strength when each person knows their spouse will absolutely refuse to give up on the relationship. When both partners make that commitment, the strength that a secure marriage offers can make all the difference during tough times. And that's when tapping into your marriage reserve tank can give you the energy to keep going. When the present is difficult, look to the past to find the strength to keep moving forward.

Closing Thoughts

For some reason, we all seem wired to look for the quick fix. We like the idea of reading a book, then practicing the recommended steps for a few weeks and experiencing lasting change without doing anything long-term. Our American culture has even figured out ways to feed into this desire for instant results. In certain cities, Amazon offers *same day* delivery on many of their items. Weight loss pills will always and forever have a certain appeal, even if they have dangerous side effects. The lottery offers everyone the chance to dream of instantly becoming rich beyond their wildest dreams. We love instant. We love shortcuts.

The problem is *life isn't like that.* But part of the appeal of these quick fix offers is that it feels good to think we might be able to permanently check off an item on our "to do" list.

Dan

Marriage, however, is definitely not an area where a quick fix is possible. In fact, I often talk to couples who are in the process of one of them making some positive changes, but the one who's made the changes is frustrated because they don't think their spouse is treating them much differently. I usually ask them how long they were controlling, deceptive, angry, manipulative, withholding, or distant. The answer is usually measured in years. Then I tell them they can't earn a difficult reputation over years and expect to erase it in a matter of weeks or months.

Change takes work. Hard, daily work. Habits and patterns are difficult to change. So your spouse will need to see the "new you" in action for a while before they can start thinking you're different from the "old you."

. . . . .

Like anything worth doing, investing in marriage daily is challenging. Again, think about the skills you use at work, in your hobbies, or in sports. Those didn't come to you immediately. You didn't snap your fingers and immediately understand how to use the Function Wizard in Microsoft Excel. You didn't pick up a remote control for a drone and instantly know how to fly it perfectly. You didn't buy yarn and darning needles and instantly know how to crochet. You didn't show up at the golf course and immediately know how to putt like your favorite pro on the PGA Tour.

But for some reason, we don't generally expect a good marriage to require the level of learning, practice, and trial-and-error basically everything else in the world requires! On some level, we all already know that. But being reminded of that truth hopefully makes us wonder how we weren't already building our lives around that reality.

We hope the simple and practical tools and suggestions in this book will inspire you to establish and consistently practice good habits. If you do, we believe you will see real change and be equipped for marriage on purpose.

Reflection Questions

Chapter 1—Make God Your Top Priority

1. Does the way you spend your time, money, or energy say something other than God is your top priority? If so, what's keeping you from making him number one?

2. Did God bring anything specific about your life or actions to your attention as you read this chapter? If so, what was it?

3. What are some specific ways you can pray for your spouse? When is the best time of day for you to pray together?

Chapter 2—Work on You

1. What steps do you need to take to work on you (regardless of whether your spouse chooses to change)?

2. Have you primarily blamed your spouse for areas of conflict? Or have you taken ownership of your contributions to miscommunications and areas of frustration? In either case, how so?

3. When have you missed seeing the 10 percent of conflict you can assume is yours to own? What can you do to work on that?

Chapter 3—Communication: Listening

1. Do you usually only *hear* your spouse? Or are you a good *listener*? How do you know?

2. What are a couple of areas where you need to improve your listening skills?

3. What is your biggest barrier to good listening (for example, a lack of focus or lack of interest)? What can you do about that?

Chapter 4—Communication: Talking

1. What is the most difficult aspect of communication for you in marriage (for example, kindness or attentiveness)? What can you do about that?

2. Would you like to see a specific hurtful word or phrase eliminated from your conversations? What is it? What can you do to make that happen?

3. How do you think you, as a couple, can build greater trust between you?

Chapter 5—Selfishness

1. What is the main way you give and receive love? What is the main way your spouse gives and receives love? If you don't know, what steps can you take to find out?

2. Do you think you've been loving your spouse the way *you* want to be loved? Or the way *they* want to be loved? How so?

3. Have you made the effort to consider what your spouse may be feeling as they're going through challenges in life? Or have you been locked in to your own perspective? How so?

Chapter 6—Forgiveness

1. Does what you've been taught about forgiveness align with the advice in this book? Explain.
2. Are you willing to ask God to help you want to *want* to forgive when you've been hurt and can't seem to get there? Why or why not?
3. What do you need to forgive your spouse for? What do you need to ask your spouse to forgive you for?

Chapter 7—Apologizing

1. How consistently do you apologize when you're in the wrong? How can you improve in that area of your marriage?
2. What are some specific areas you need to take responsibility for in your marriage? Why do you think you haven't taken responsibility for them?
3. Are your apologies genuine? Or are they non-apologies? How can you make your apologies more genuine?

Chapter 8—Differences

1. What small differences of opinion or different habits cause friction in your marriage? When you say them out loud, do they sound less significant? What does that tell you?

2. Have you identified your "irreconcilable differences" as a couple? If so, how do you manage them?

3. How can you compromise in one specific area of difference that has tripped you up in the past?

Chapter 9—Staying Connected

1. Why do you think spending time together is important for couples?

2. What are some activities you used to enjoy together and can get back to doing?

3. What financial, relational, or spiritual goals do you think you should address as a couple? What plan can you make to accomplish setting those goals?

NOTES

1. Randall Munroe, "Soul Mates," https://what-if.xkcd.com/9/.

2. To learn more about listening to God and read some of the stories from Mary Geegh that originally inspired Dan to start listening to him, look for her book *God Guides* for sale on the Winning At Home website at winningathome.com or on Amazon.

3. Thomas à Kempis, *The Imitation of Christ* (Peabody, MA: Hendrickson Publishers, 2004), 16.

4. Timothy Keller (with Kathy Keller), *The Meaning of Marriage* (New York: Penguin Books, 2011), 87.

5. C. S. Lewis, *The Problem of Pain* (San Francisco: HarperOne, 1940), 35.

6. "*hamartano,*" Henry George Liddell and Robert Scott, *Greek-English Lexicon* (Oxford: Clarendon Press, 1996), 77.

7. Henry Cloud and John Townsend, *Boundaries* (Grand Rapids, MI: Zondervan, 2008), 265.

8. Malcolm Gladwell, *Outliers* (New York: Little, Brown and Company, 2008), 42.

9. Sam Harris, *Lying* (United States: Four Elephants Press, 2013), 41.

10. Howard Markman, Scott Stanley, and Susan Blumberg, *Fighting for Your Marriage* (San Francisco: Jossey-Bass, 2010), 37.

11. Gretchen Rubin, *The Happiness Project* (New York: HarperCollins, 2018), 48.

12. Judith Wallerstein and Sandra Blakeslee, *The Good Marriage* (New York: Houghton Mifflin Harcourt, 1995), 17.

13. Gary Chapman, *The 5 Love Languages* (Chicago: Northfield Publishing, 2015), 202.

14. Cloud and Townsend, *Boundaries*, 268.

15. Peter Newhouse, *Winning the Battle Over Abuse* (Zeeland, MI: Winning At Home, 2012), 87.

16. Donald E. Gowan, *The Bible on Forgiveness* (Eugene, OR: Pickwick Publications, 2010), 200.

17. Pierre Eade, *Our Good Father* (Newberry, FL: Bridge-Logos, 2017), 67.

18. Newhouse, *Winning the Battle Over Abuse*, 87.

19. A. C. Grayling, *Meditations for the Humanist: Ethics for a Secular Age* (London: Oxford University Press, 2002), 57.

20. Alan Seaborn, *Marriage: Five Years Later* (Zeeland, MI: Winning At Home, 2019), 26.

OTHER TITLES FROM WINNING AT HOME

All titles are available at
winningathome.com

Once-A-Day: Nurturing Great Kids Devotional
365 Practical Insights for Parenting with Grace

By Dan Seaborn

The Necessary Nine
How to Stay Happily Married for Life!

By Dan Seaborn &
Dr. Peter Newhouse
with Lisa Velthouse

Journeying with Pain
Finding Hope When You Don't Find Answers

By Alan Seaborn

Winning the Battle Over Abuse
A Self-Directed Guide to Healing

By Dr. Peter Newhouse

One-Minute Reflections for Couples:
Marriage Rendezvous, Stay Married for Life, Two to One, Leaving a Legacy

By Dan Seaborn & Dr. Peter Newhouse with Susan Lewis

Marriage: Five Years Later
Lessons From the Early Years

By Alan Seaborn

Prescriptions for Healthy Relationships

By Dr. Peter Newhouse

SUPPORTING MARRIAGES & FAMILIES THROUGH

Counseling Services

Our staff of licensed professionals counsel individuals, couples, and families, helping them to overcome barriers and develop toward wholeness. We offer counseling for married couples, premarital couples, single parents, adoptive and blended families, divorce recovery, mood disorders, communication issues, domestic violence situations, and so much more. We have counselors who work with adults as well as children and adolescents.

Coaching Services

We have a team of certified coaches who can provide the guidance you need when you get stuck in a certain area of your life or relationships or you just need help pushing forward in meeting goals or clarifying your purpose in life. We provide individual and marriage coaching, group or team coaching, as well as corporate and leadership coaching.

Community Events

Community events are a unique opportunity for us to combine the strength of community with the joy of relationships. Whether to support our mission or strengthen bonds of trust and love in relationships, our events are done in creative and fun ways that make the information easy to receive, retain, and carry through in relationships.

Speakers

Our speakers strive to bring a message of love, hope, peace, and unity to individuals, marriages, and families through whatever topic is addressed. Their goal is to motivate audiences to thought, reflection, and often action, as needed, to help participants achieve their ultimate desired outcomes or reach some helpful conclusions to move forward.

Winning At Home

LOCATIONS

Zeeland - Holland - Tampa Bay

For more information about our services, visit

WINNINGATHOME.COM

1-888-924-8326

Winning At Home encourages people at
all ages and stages of family development
to lead Christ-centered homes.